THE OFFICIAL

ENGLAND RUGBY

MISCELLANY

ENGLAND
RUGBY

BY STUART FARMER

VSP

Vision Sports Publishing
2 Coombe Gardens,
London, SW20 0QU

www.visionsp.co.uk

This Third Edition Published by
Vision Sports Publishing in 2008

ISBN-13: 978-1-905326-43-3

Text © Vision Sports Publishing Limited
© 2008 Rugby Football Union. Licensed by Copyright Promotions

Written by Stuart Farmer

Printed and bound by GGP Media, Pössneck

Typeset by Palimpsest Book Production Limited,
Grangemouth, Stirlingshire

A CIP catalogue record for this book is
available from the British Library

Mixed Sources
Product group from well-managed
forests and other controlled sources
www.fsc.org Cert no. SGS-COC-1940
© 1996 Forest Stewardship Council
FSC

Vision Sports Publishing are
proud that this book is made
from paper certified by the
Forest Stewardship Council

— FOREWORD—

By Martin Johnson

It's a great pleasure for me to write the introduction to this book which is full of facts, trivia and quirky stories about the England rugby team. Call me a 'statto' if you like, but I find all of that kind of thing very interesting.

Having said that, I was never particularly concerned about trying to set or beat records myself. Some people said I should carry on and try to play 100 test matches, but if you're doing that you're playing for the wrong reasons. Whenever you play for England, you want to justify your selection by your performance, and the number of caps you have has no bearing on that.

I trained a long, long time before I achieved my ambition of playing for England, so making my international debut was a momentous occasion. It was a proud moment for me to pull on the white jersey for the first time against France in 1993. But more than pride, I felt anxiety. Once you get there it's all well and good because you've put the shirt on, but you want to do yourself justice. That feeling carries on even to your last game – you don't ever want to let the team or yourself down.

In my England career I enjoyed numerous highlights, many of which get a mention inside these pages: beating the All Blacks at Twickenham in 1993; winning the Grand Slam in 1995; winning the World Cup quarter-final against Australia in 1995; our first southern hemisphere win under Sir Clive Woodward against South Africa at Twickenham in 1998, which ended their record run of unbeaten test matches; winning the Grand Slam in 2003 and, obviously, lifting the World Cup as England captain later that same year.

Partly because we play more test matches now than they did in the past, the guys I played with in those sides set lots of individual records that appear in the book. Jason Leonard's caps, Rory Underwood's tries, Jonny Wilkinson's points – these three records in particular will take some beating.

As well as giving all the records, results and stats, this book is crammed full of fascinating stories about England's rugby history – a history that goes back over 130 years to the first ever international. I already knew that Scotland were our first opponents but what I didn't realise, until now, is that the game was 20-a-side! There are loads of other tidbits of intriguing information like that here. I especially liked the story of the guy who was selected for a game by mistake because he had a similar name to another player. Then there was the unfortunate player who scored a hat-trick of tries on his England debut but didn't get picked again. The story that surprised me most, though, was the one of the player in the late nineteenth century who travelled from the West Country to play in London every weekend and had to walk the last ten miles home. I just found that incredible.

I'm sure that all England fans, especially those who are interested in the history of the game, will enjoy dipping in and out of these pages. Stuart Farmer, who has written this book, used to work at Leicester, my old club. It was a bit of a joke among the players that if you wanted to find out any rugby stat, then Stuart was the man to ring! He certainly knows his subject.

Martin Johnson CBE

— ACKNOWLEDGEMENTS —

I would like to thank a number of individuals who have aided immeasurably in the production of this book.

To Richard Prescott the RFU Communications Director and media officer of England Rugby and Paul Morgan the editor of Rugby World magazine who initiated my involvement in this project.

To Jed Smith, the curator of the Museum of Rugby, Twickenham, for his knowledge and hospitality during my visits. To John Jenkins for his continuing work in verifying birth records of international rugby players. To John Griffiths for his pioneering work in the research of England international rugby. To a worldwide network of superb rugby statisticians and historians including New Zealand's Geoff Miller, Fiji's Jeremy Duxbury, Argentina's Frankie Deges, Nick Cross and Rugby League's Robert Gate.

To Brian and Gillian Bates for their enduring friendship and unstinting dedication to building the databases and agreeing to always take on my research work with my ridiculous deadlines. To my wife and business partner Janet for her love, understanding and diligence.

Finally to the top class team at Vision Sports Publishing, including Jim Drewett and his colleague Toby Trotman for entrusting me with the project.

As with all books of this type the odd omission and inaccuracy may appear. If any reader has any further information, which may be of use, would they please contact the author through the publishers?

Happy delving

Stuart Farmer

— AUTHOR'S NOTES —

The term 'international' refers to an international match in which a country awards caps. Occasionally we have used 'test match' to refer to the same criteria even though strictly speaking the term is an Australian one which has never been fully accepted in England.

Where appearances are marked thus (25+3) it means that a player has started 25 capped matches and been a replacement who had some game time in three further matches. Any caps gained for the British & Irish Lions or their forerunners are not included.

Players are referred to throughout by the names and nicknames they were known by during their playing careers: ie) 'Jenny' Greenwood for John Eric Greenwood, and 'Cherry' Pillman for Charles Henry Pillman etc.

Any statistics pertaining to club representation take account only of the club that player was appearing for at the time of his cap, and not any other clubs he may have appeared for before or after the dates of his England career.

All stats in the *Official England Rugby Miscellany* are correct up until July 2008.

Up until 1875, international rugby matches were decided by the number of 'goals' scored (conversions and dropped goals), but from 1876 the number of tries scored could be used to decide a match if teams were level on goals. The scoring of 'points' was not formally introduced until the late 1880s, a try scoring one point, a conversion two and a drop goal three. Various experiments were tried until 1890/91, when the International Rugby Board's system was adopted to make points scoring uniform in international matches. This was in an attempt to cure inconsistencies which meant, for instance, that when England visited Scotland in 1890 their two tries were worth two points each under SRU laws, but two weeks later against Ireland at Blackheath, England's three tries were worth just one point each under RFU laws!

Below is a table denoting the changes in the scoring systems over the years:

Era	Try	Conversion	Drop Goal	Penalty Goal	Goal/Mark
1890/91	1	2	3	2	3
1891/92 to 1892/93	2	3	4	3	4
1893/94 to 1904/05	3	2	4	3	4
1905/06 to 1947/48	3	2	4	3	3
1948/49 to 1970/71	3	2	3	3	3
1971/72 to 1976/77	4	2	3	3	3
1977/78 to 1991/92	4	2	3	3	Void
1992/93 to date	5	2	3	3	Void

— ENGLAND RUGBY TIMELINE —

26 Jan 1871	The RFU is founded in London by 21 local clubs.
27 Mar 1871	Scotland beat England in the first-ever international match at the Academy Ground, Raeburn Place, Edinburgh, in front of a crowd of 4000. Each team fields 20 players – Scotland win by one goal and one try to one try.
15 Feb 1875	England beat Ireland by a goal and a try to nil in the first international between the two sides at the Oval cricket ground, London.
13 Dec 1875	England beat Ireland by a goal and a try to nil in the first international to be played in Ireland at Leinster Cricket Ground, Rathmines, Dublin.
5 Feb 1877	Ireland and England appear in the first international to feature 15 players a side, at the Oval, London. England win by two goals and two tries to nil.
10 Mar 1879	The first Calcutta Cup match between Scotland and England ends in a draw at Raeburn Place.
16 Dec 1882	In what is now regarded as the first International Championship (later Five Nations) match, England beat Wales by two goals and four tries to nil at St Helen's, Swansea.
3 Mar 1883	England's victory over Scotland gives them their first 'Triple Crown' in the inaugural International Championship.
1 Mar 1884	A disputed try by England in a match at Blackheath eventually leads to Scotland's refusal to play them again in internationals between 1887–1890.
1886	The first meeting of the International Rugby Football Board takes place in Manchester. England declines to join until 1890.
29 Aug 1895	Twenty clubs resign from the RFU and form the Northern Union (later the Rugby League).
22 Mar 1906	England defeat France 35–8 in the first international between the two sides at Parc des Princes in Paris.
15 Jan 1910	England beat Wales 11–6 in the first international at Twickenham, London, the new home of English rugby football.
4 Jan 1913	England lose their first match at Twickenham, by a score of 9–3 to the touring Springboks.
13 Apr 1914	England claim their second Grand Slam in succession with a 38–13 win over France at Stade Colombes in Paris.

2

1914–18	111 rugby internationals lose their lives during World War I, including 27 England internationals.
21 Jan 1922	Both teams wear numbers in an international for the first time when Wales thrash England 28–6 at Cardiff Arms Park, running in eight tries.
21 Mar 1925	Scotland defeat England 14–11 in the first international match at Murrayfield, Edinburgh. The win is their first over England since 1912 and also completes their first Grand Slam.
15 Jan 1927	England beat Wales 11–5 at Twickenham, the first match to be broadcast on BBC radio.
6 Apr 1931	France beat England 14–13 in Paris in their last match in the Five Nations Championship before being expelled from the tournament until 1947 following accusations of professionalism.
4 Jan 1936	England inflict a second consecutive test loss on New Zealand, 13–0 at Twickenham, following the All Blacks' 12–13 defeat to Wales two weeks previously.
18 Mar 1939	England beat Scotland 9–6 at Murrayfield, Edinburgh, in the last international before the outbreak of World War II.
3 Jan 1948	Australia beat England 11–0 at Twickenham, winning three and losing one of their four internationals against the home nations. The Wallabies become the first touring team to the UK not to concede a try in any test.
4 Jun 1963	England's first overseas tour to Australia and New Zealand ends with losses in all three internationals.
20 Dec 1969	England beat South Africa 11–8 at Twickenham to record their first ever win over the Springboks.
18 Mar 1972	England's 23–9 loss to Scotland is the first time they have lost all four championship matches in a single season; they finish with the outright wooden spoon and a whitewash.
15 Sep 1973	England defeat New Zealand 16–10 in a one-off test in Auckland – their first test win in New Zealand.
1982	Former England internationals Bill Beaumont and Fran Cotton announce they will accept royalties from books on the sport and are later expelled from the "administration, organisation or control of rugby football".
4 Nov 1989	Rory Underwood becomes the second England player

	to score five tries in an international when England humble Fiji 58–23 at Twickenham.
7 Mar 1992	England defeat Wales 24–0 at Twickenham to claim their second consecutive Grand Slam.
17 Oct 1992	England defeat Canada 26–13 in the first international between the two sides, and the first full international rugby union match at Wembley Stadium.
26 Aug 1995	Rugby Union becomes "open" for the first time during a meeting at the Concorde Hotel in Paris.
6 Dec 1997	England and New Zealand draw 26–26 at Twickenham, the then highest score for any drawn test match.
30 Mar 2003	England claim their 12th Grand Slam but their first in the expanded Six Nations Championship with a 42–6 win over Ireland at Lansdowne Road in Dublin.
22 Nov 2003	England become world champions, beating Australia 20–17 after extra time in the fifth Rugby World Cup final at Stadium Australia, Sydney.
20 Oct 2007	England narrowly fail to defend their World Champion's crown as they fall to South Africa 15–6 in the final of the 2007 Rugby World Cup.

— THE RUGBY SCHOOL GAME —

By the early 1800s, various forms of football were being played at England's major public schools, each with their own distinctive set of rules (or lack of them!).

There is an account of one such game being played at the famous Rugby School as early as 1817. The match was contested at Old Bigside, the name of the field, between teams of 40 players or more. The rules were few and simple; touch was marked out on the sides of the ground and no-one was allowed to run towards the opposition goal with the ball in his grasp.

However, as the famous legend goes, during one of these games in 1823, 16-year-old Rugby schoolboy William Webb Ellis is said to have "caught the ball up in his arms, and instead of retiring back or punting forward as the rules demanded, rushed forward with the ball in his hands towards the opposite goal".

The game of Rugby was born, and by 1841 the technique of "running in", as it became known, was legalised in Rugby School's version of the game providing that, (a) the ball was caught "on the bound", (b) the catcher was not "off his side", and (c) that the catcher did not pass the ball but ran on himself.

Amidst growing confusion and disputes over the varying rules of football adopted by different schools and clubs, on 28 August 1845, Rugby School drew up its first set of 37 codified rules. These included:

Hacking [kicking or tripping an opponent] is permitted, but not above the knee. Holding a player carrying the ball is permitted, but with one arm only. "Running in" is permitted, but passing with the hands is banned. And if no decision is reached after five afternoons' play, a match will be declared drawn.

The Rugby game featured goals, with posts and a crossbar, much like those used today, whilst up until the late 1850s, only those who had been awarded school caps were allowed to take part in the play (the origin of the custom of awarding caps in both rugby and football today).

William Webb Ellis: source of rugby's 'creationist' myth

— A UNION IS BORN —

Following numerous disputes over the different rules adopted by different schools and clubs, in October 1863 the Football Association was formed and the first ever uniform set of rules was laid out.

However, these rules outlawed players running with the ball in their hand – the essence of the Rugby School rules that had been adopted by many clubs – and many refused to join the Football Association, continuing instead to play the game their way. Eventually, on the evening of 26 January 1871, a party of 32 London and suburban football clubs that had agreed to follow the Rugby School laws assembled at Pall Mall Restaurant, Cockspur Street, London and, under the presidency of EC Holmes, captain of the Richmond Club, they resolved unanimously to form what they called the Rugby Football Union.

The clubs drafted a set of bye laws, elected a president, Algernon Rutter, and a secretary and treasurer, Edwin H Ash, both of Richmond, along with a committee of 13 who were entrusted to draw up the laws of the game upon the basis of the code in use at Rugby School.

The names of the clubs present on this auspicious occasion were:

Blackheath, Richmond, Wellington College, Guy's Hospital, Harlequins, King's College, St Paul's School, Civil Service, Marlborough Nomads, West Kent, Wimbledon Hornets, Gipsies, Clapham Rovers, Law, Flamingoes, Queen's House, Lausanne, Addison, Ravenscourt Park, Mohicans and Belsize Park.

The first nine clubs are still in existence, whilst the other 12 are either defunct or evolved into different clubs. Clapham Rovers switched over to playing football and won the FA Cup in 1880. Belsize Park moved to become Rosslyn Park in 1879, and were reformed in 1971. Marlborough Nomads merged with Rosslyn Park in 1911, and Queen's House were from Greenwich.

Legend has it that Wasps (formed in 1867 and currently London Wasps) should have attended the meeting but went to the wrong restaurant!

— LIST OF FOES —

Here is a list of all England's 21 different opponents in official test matches, and their record against each:

Opponent	First met	P	W	D	L
Scotland	27 Mar 1871	125	66	17	42
Ireland	15 Feb 1875	121	70	8	43
Wales	19 Feb 1881	117	53	12	52
New Zealand Natives	16 Feb 1889	1	1	-	-
New Zealand	2 Dec 1905	31	6	1	24
France	22 Mar 1906	91	49	7	35
South Africa	8 Dec 1906	30	12	1	17
Australia*	9 Jan 1909	35	14	1	20
RFU President's XV	17 Apr 1971	1	-	-	1
Argentina	30 May 1981	12	8	1	3
Romania	5 Jan 1985	4	4	-	-
Japan	30 May 1987	1	1	-	-
United States	3 Jun 1987	5	5	-	-
Fiji	16 Jun 1988	4	4	-	-
Italy	8 Oct 1991	14	14	-	-
Canada	17 Oct 1992	6	6	-	-
Western Samoa#	4 Jun 1995	5	5	-	-
Netherlands	14 Nov 1998	1	1	-	-
Tonga	15 Oct 1999	2	2	-	-
Georgia	12 Oct 2003	1	1	-	-
Uruguay	2 Nov 2003	1	1	-	-

* including the 18–11 win over New South Wales at Twickenham on 7 January 1928.
#Western Samoa became simply Samoa in 1998.
(stats correct up to July 2008)

— THE PIONEERS —

The first ever international rugby match kicked off at 3pm at the Academy Ground, Raeburn Place, in Edinburgh on Monday, 27 March 1871. The game was played in front of 4,000 spectators with 20 players on each side, with each half lasting 50 minutes, on a pitch measuring 120 yards by 55 yards. There was to be no "hacking" or tripping up, and the ball was not allowed to be picked up for a run unless it was "absolutely bounding", in other words bouncing off the ground as opposed to rolling.

England, skippered by Blackheath's Frederic Stokes, lined up with players from ten different clubs, but lost the match by one try to a goal and a try.

The teams:

Scotland	England
William Brown (Glasgow Academicals)	Arthur Lyon (Liverpool)
Thomas Chalmers (Glasgow Academicals)	Arthur Guillemard (West Kent)
Alfred Clunies-Ross (St Andrew's Uni)	Richard Osborne (Manchester)
Thomas Marshall (Edinburgh Academicals)	William MacLaren (Manchester)
William Cross (Merchistonians)	Frank Tobin (Liverpool)
John Arthur (Glasgow Academicals)	John Bentley (Gipsies)
Francis Moncreiff (capt, Edinburgh Academicals)	Joseph Green (West Kent)
William Lyall (Edinburgh Academicals)	Frederic Stokes (capt, Blackheath)
J.S. Thomson (St Andrew's Uni)	Charles Sherrard (Blackheath)
Bulldog Irvine (Edinburgh Academicals)	Benjamin Burns (Blackheath)
Alexander Robertson (West of Scotland)	Charles Crompton (Blackheath)
James Finlay (Edinburgh Academicals)	Alfred Davenport (Ravenscourt Park)
George Ritchie (Merchistonians)	John Dugdale (Ravenscourt Park)
Angus Buchanan (Royal HSFP)	Arthur Gibson (Manchester)
Robert Munro (St Andrew's Uni)	H.J.C. Turner (Manchester)
Andrew Colville (Merchistonians)	Reginald Birkett (Clapham Rovers)
Daniel Drew (Glasgow Academicals)	John Clayton (Liverpool)
J. Forsyth (Edinburgh University)	Alf Hamersley (Marlborough Nomads)
James Mein (Edinburgh Academicals)	John Luscombe (Gipsies)
John MacFarlane (Edinburgh University)	Dawson Turner (Manchester)

The standard of moustaches in the England squad has gone downhill since the late 1800s

— THE GREAT SPLIT —

By 1893 there had been a growing feeling, particularly in the north, that players should be allowed "broken time" payments to recompense them for time taken off work in order to play rugby football. However, at the Rugby Football Union's Annual General Meeting on 20 September 1893 a motion to legalise professionalism was defeated by 282 votes to 136.

This in turn brought about the formation of the Northern Union (later the Rugby League) on 29 August 1895 at the George Hotel in Huddersfield, where 20 clubs from Lancashire, Yorkshire and Cheshire resigned from the RFU to join the new Union: Batley, Bradford, Brighouse Rangers, Broughton Rangers, Halifax, Huddersfield, Hull, Hunslet, Leeds, Leigh, Liversedge, Manningham, Oldham, Rochdale Hornets, St Helens, Tyldesley, Wakefield Trinity, Warrington, Widnes and Wigan.

It was not until 1906 that the new organisation reduced the number of players from 15 to 13 per side, and 1922 when it took the name of the Rugby Football League.

— NEVER ON A SUNDAY —

England didn't play a test match on a Sunday until 29 May 1988 at Ballymore in Brisbane where they lost out 16–22 to the Wallabies. The second test of that series at Concord Oval in Sydney a week later was also played on the Sabbath.

The first Five Nations Sunday match was played between Scotland and England at Murrayfield on 22 March 1998 with England winning 34–20, and England's first Sunday home game was played at McAlpine Stadium in Huddersfield on 22 November 1998 when they took on Italy in a World Cup qualifying game and won 23–15. Twickenham's first Sunday international was also for the visit of Italy in the Six Nations Championship on 9 March 2003.

— TURNCOATS —

Four full England internationals have also been capped for another country:

James Marsh, who was a three-quarter back, first turned out for Scotland in two games in 1889 against Wales and Ireland. Marsh then went on to make his one and only appearance for England against Ireland at Manchester on 6 February 1892. Marsh thus has the unique distinction of having turned out for two different nations in the International Championship.

Frank Mellish was born in South Africa but gained six caps for England between 1920–21, before returning home and going on to win six Springbok caps between 1921–24, the first of which came just six months after representing England for the last time.

Barry Holmes gained four caps for England in 1949 and was then awarded two for Argentina later the same year. Indeed, he played against France three times in six months for two different countries!

Hong Kong-born centre **Jamie Salmon** was capped for New Zealand on three occasions in 1981 during the All Blacks tour of Europe, before making his England debut against New Zealand in Christchurch in 1985 and going on to gain a dozen England caps over the next two years.

— BLUE PETERS —

England's first black player was James Peters, a one-time dockyard worker at Devonport, who was born in Salford in 1879, and who was capped for the first time at fly-half against Scotland at Inverleith on 17 March 1906 aged 26. James went on to gain five caps, scoring two tries before eventually signing to play rugby league for Barrow in 1913. Peters had been educated at Knowle School in Bristol and played his senior rugby for Plymouth.

— DON'T OVER TRAIN —

Leigh-born Frank Wright, a pupil at Edinburgh Academy, only won his single cap for England against Scotland at Raeburn Place, Edinburgh on 19 March 1881 because half-back Henry Taylor of Blackheath missed the train to Edinburgh!

— FOOTSTEP FOLLOWERS —

Father and son combinations who have both played for England.

Name	Father	Son(s)
Milton	William (2 caps, 1874–75)	John (5 caps, 1904–07) & Cecil (1 cap, 1906)
Birkett	Reginald (4 caps, 1871–77)	John (21 caps, 1906–12)
Tucker	William (5 caps, 1894–95)	Bill (3 caps, 1926–30)
Wilkinson	Harry J. (1 cap, 1889)	Harry (4 caps, 1929–30)
Hubbard	George (2 caps, 1892)	John (1 cap, 1930)
Hobbs	Reginald F.A. (2 caps, 1899–1903)	Reginald G.S. (4 caps, 1932)
Weston	Henry (1 cap, 1901)	William (16 caps, 1933–38)
Scott	Frank (1 cap, 1907)	Edward (5 caps, 1947–48)
Preece	Ivor (12 caps, 1948–51)	Peter (12 caps, 1972–76)
Greenwood	Dick (5 caps, 1966–69)	Will (55 caps, 1997–2005)
Fidler	John (4 caps, 1981–84)	Rob (2 caps, 1998)

— TWENTY-TWENTY —

England's first eight international matches, between 1871 and 1876, were all contested by teams of 20 players a side, with as many as 14 of those being forwards.

On 5 February 1877 at the Oval, England participated in the first international match with the modern number of 15 players a side, against Ireland, although the formations were vastly different to today with both teams fielding two full backs, two three-quarters, two half-backs and a pack of nine forwards. Later, one of the full-backs moved into the three-quarter line and the backs formation stayed this way until 1893.

On 6 January 1894 at Birkenhead Park England copied the Welsh example of playing four three-quarters for the first time, overran the Welsh 24–3, and kept this composition of two wings and two centres until this very day.

— FLYING PRINCE —

Prince Alexander Obolensky, the son of Prince Alexis of Russia, was born in St Petersburg on 17 February 1916. He was brought to England aged one and later educated at Trent College and Brasenose College, Oxford.

The only Russian Prince ever to play for England

As a 19-year-old he famously made his debut for England in 1936 against the touring All Blacks and starred with two wonder tries in a 13–0 unexpected defeat of New Zealand. He won four caps in successive matches that year before going on tour with the British Isles team to Argentina, scoring 29 tries in just seven appearances including a record 17 in one game against Brazil.

When World War II broke out "Obo" joined the Royal Air Force, tragically becoming the first rugby international to lose his life in the conflict when his Hawker Hurricane crash-landed at Martlesham Heath airfield in East Anglia. He was just 24 years old when he died, and remains the only east European born England player.

— TWO WILLIAM TUCKERS —

Two players with exactly the same name have turned out for England, the father and son duo of William Eldon Tucker senior and junior. Tucker senior was a forward who was born in Bermuda and educated in Canada and at Cambridge University. He won five caps for England between 1894–1895.

His son William junior was also born in Bermuda and educated at Sherborne School and Cambridge University. A number eight forward, he won three caps between 1926–1930.

— EASTER EGG CHASERS —

England have played just eight matches in their history at Easter, all coincidentally in the Five Nations Championship away to France, and all on Easter Monday – in 1912, 1914, 1921, 1923, 1925, 1929, 1931 and 1948.

— RARE TUESDAY —

England have played at least one test match on every day of the week. The most popular day is, predictably, a Saturday with 425 matches. There have however been just two games on a Tuesday: during the 1963 tour of New Zealand and Australia, England played their only test against the Wallabies at Sydney Sports Ground on 4 June and lost 9–18. In the 1991 World Cup they also met Italy on a Tuesday at Twickenham and won 36–6.

— ENGLAND LEGENDS: ROB ANDREW —

Appointed as the RFU's elite director of rugby in 2006, Rob Andrew will long be remembered as the player who dropped the winning goal in the World Cup quarter-final against Australia in Cape Town in 1995. But his achievements in the game go well beyond this single memorable moment.

Andrew is still England's most capped fly-half of all time and finished his test career as his country's top international points scorer, although his tally of 396 points has since been surpassed by his protégé at Newcastle, Jonny Wilkinson.

Andrew made his test debut against Romania in 1985, slotting 18 points from four penalties and two dropped goals, but for many years he was regarded as too inconsistent to be England's front-line goal kicker. However, with the retirement of Jonathan Webb, Andrew was permanently handed the penalty-taking role in 1994. After completely remodelling his kicking technique, he went on to break almost every England record.

An accomplished cricketer, Andrew played for Cambridge University in the Varsity match in both rugby and cricket, and scored a first-class century (101 not out) against Nottinghamshire in 1984.

With the advent of professionalism in 1995, he joined Newcastle from Wasps as their first director of rugby and won the Premiership at his first attempt in season 1997–98. In August 2006 Andrew took up the newly created post of the RFU's elite director of rugby, overseeing all aspects of professional rugby in England.

Rob Andrew: England's most capped fly-half

Christopher Robert Andrew MBE Factfile
Born: 18 Feb 1963 in Richmond, Yorkshire
Clubs: Middlesbrough, Nottingham, Gordon (Australia), Wasps,
Toulouse (France), Newcastle Falcons
Caps: 71 (W50, D2, L19)
Scoring: 2T, 33C, 86PG, 21DG – 396 points
England debut: 5 Jan 1985 vs Romania (Twickenham)

— OFF THE BENCH —

The most caps won by an England player coming off the replacements
bench is Matt Dawson with 22, Martin Corry follows him with 21
including five instances of him winning a cap only as a blood replacement.
The list continues with Joe Worsley 21, Danny Grewcock 18, Simon
Shaw, Lewis Moody and Austin Healey all on 14 replacement
appearances. The most caps off the bench won by a player who has never
started an England test is Sale's Andy Titterrell with four, whilst Mike
Worsley and Neil McCarthy all have three caps without ever having
started a test match.

— UNUSUAL OPPONENTS —

England have played just three full test matches against teams who
were not representing a whole country:

- On 16 February 1889 at Blackheath they faced the New Zealand
  Natives, who were effectively forerunners of the Maori team.
  England won 7–0.
- On 7 January 1928 England played New South Wales Waratahs
  in a match later recognised as a full test match by the Australian
  Rugby Union because Queensland had withdrawn from the ARU
  in the 1920s. England won 18–11.
- On 17 April 1971 at Twickenham England took on an RFU President's
  XV to celebrate the centenary of the RFU. Of the 15 overseas players
  who turned out for the President's XV in their 28–11 victory, just
  two never played against England for their countries: Australian centre
  Stephen Knight and All Black fly-half Wayne Cottrell.

— ALCOCK-UP —

Dr Arnold Alcock, the Guy's Hospital hooker, was surprisingly selected to play for England against South Africa at Crystal Palace on 8 December 1906. However, embarrassed RFU officials discovered he had been incorrectly named instead of Liverpool's Andrew Slocock.

As it was too late to rectify the error, Alcock made his one and only England appearance in the 3–3 draw. Slocock played in England's next match, eventually making eight appearances in all.

— DANGEROUS DAN —

New Zealand first five eighth Dan Carter has a phenomenal scoring record against England, racking up his 120 point haul in just six appearances for an impressive 20 points a test average. The only other player to have tallied over 100 points against England in test matches is Wallaby legend Michael Lynagh who scored 108 points in 8 matches between 1984–95.

The full list of those who have scored 50 points against England in tests is:

Player	Country	Tries	Conv	Pens	Drops	Points	Apps
Dan Carter	New Zealand	4	20	20	-	120	6
Michael Lynagh	Australia	2	14	24	-	108	8
Percy Montgomery	South Africa	1	20	18	-	99	12
Andrew Mehrtens	New Zealand	1	19	13	1	85	6+2
Ronan O'Gara	Ireland	1	8	17	2	78	5+3
Matthew Burke	Australia	4	9	12	-	74	6+1
Neil Jenkins	Wales	-	7	16	1	65	10
Gavin Hastings	Scotland	-	4	19	-	65	10
Dimitri Yachvili	France	1	3	18	-	65	5+1
Chris Paterson	Scotland	-	5	17	-	61	9
Gonzalo Quesada	Argentina	1	3	15	1	59	5
Braam van Straaten	South Africa	1	-	17	-	56	4
Andy Irvine	Scotland	1	7	12	-	54	10
Diego Dominguez	Italy	1	8	9	1	51	7

— TRY, TRY AGAIN —

The most tries scored against England in a career is nine, by prolific Scottish wing Ian Smith during a dazzling spell of five successive appearances against the Auld Enemy between 1926 and 1932.

Next on the list is All Black giant Jonah Lomu with eight tries and Australian speedster Ben Tune with seven. New Zealand dual cricket and rugby international Jeff Wilson and three legendary Welshmen, Gerald Davies, Dewi Bebb and Willie Llewellyn, are next in line with six apiece.

— CHASING JASON —

With Jason Leonard leading the pack as the only player ever to record more than 100 caps, here's the full list of men who have played 50 times or more for England:

	Player	Career	Caps	St+Rep	Ar	Au	Fr	Ir	It	NZ	SA	Sc	Wa	Oth
1	Jason Leonard	1990–2004	114	102+12	6	9	18	13	9	7	12	14	13	13
2=	Rory Underwood	1984–1996	85	85+0	2	8	15	14	2	3	4	12	14	11
2=	Lawrence Dallaglio	1995–2007	85	70+15	2	9	13	7	8	7	10	9	10	10
4	Martin Johnson	1993–2003	84	82+2	3	8	13	8	6	7	9	9	9	12
5	Matt Dawson	1995–2006	77	55+22	1	9	9	8	9	8	6	9	10	8
6	Mike Catt	1994–2007	75	62+13	4	12	12	5	4	3	9	5	11	10
7	Will Carling	1988–1997	72	72+0	5	5	12	11	2	3	4	11	10	9
8=	Rob Andrew	1985–1997	71	69+2	2	6	12	11	2	3	3	10	11	11
8=	Richard Hill	1997–2005	71	68+3	1	10	10	7	7	7	8	7	8	6
10	Jonny Wilkinson	1998–2008	70	66+4	1	8	11	8	7	4	9	7	8	7
11	Danny Grewcock	1997–2007	69	51+18	3	6	6	7	8	7	9	9	8	6
12	Joe Worsley	1999–2007	67	44+23	1	7	9	6	6	5	8	7	8	10
13	Neil Back	1994–2005	66	63+3	2	7	8	7	6	5	9	7	7	8
14	Jerry Guscott	1989–1999	65	62+3	3	5	10	9	4	3	3	9	8	11
15=	Brian Moore	1987–1995	64	63+1	3	7	10	9	2	3	3	10	9	8
15=	Phil Vickery	1998–2008	64	56+8	2	8	9	5	4	6	9	5	8	8
15=	Martin Corry	1996–2007	64	43+21	4	5	12	5	7	3	8	4	7	9
18	Ben Kay	2001–2008	60	48+12	2	6	9	5	5	5	8	6	6	9
19	Peter Winterbottom	1982–1993	58	58+0	3	4	11	8	1	2	3	10	11	5
20	Ben Cohen	2000–2006	57	54+3	2	6	10	5	5	6	6	6	7	4
21	Mike Tindall	2000–2008	56	52+4	1	7	7	5	5	7	7	5	7	5
22=	Wade Dooley	1985–1993	55	54+1	3	5	9	9	-	2	1	9	10	7
22=	Will Greenwood	1997–2005	55	50+5	1	6	7	5	6	4	7	5	6	8
22=	Josh Lewsey	1998–2007	55	53+2	1	6	10	4	4	6	6	5	3	10
25	Graham Rowntree	1995–2006	54	47+7	1	6	6	6	7	3	3	5	5	12
26	Lewis Moody	2001–2008	53	39+14	2	6	7	4	3	3	8	2	6	12
27=	Kyran Bracken	1993–2003	51	38+13	2	5	7	6	5	4	5	5	5	7
27=	Austin Healey	1997–2003	51	37+14	-	7	5	5	5	6	8	4	5	6
27=	Jason Robinson	2001–2007	51	47+4	-	6	10	5	4	2	7	5	6	6

— ENGLAND LEGENDS: CLIVE WOODWARD —

Although best known for his coaching exploits with the World Cup winning England team, Clive Woodward was also one of the most elusive post-war centres to play for his country. An expansive player in an otherwise cautious team, his talents were shown to masterful effect in the deciding Grand Slam victory over Scotland in 1980.

Born into a services family, Woodward was first selected to play in a Welsh schools trial but had to withdraw through injury. He graduated instead through England colts, under-23 and B levels, until making his full England debut as a replacement against Ireland in 1980.

Woodward embarked on his highly successful coaching career in 1990, assisting Oxford in their preparations for the university match. Later, he went on to coach Henley, taking them to the National Leagues for the first time in the 1994–95 season. His innovative 'flat ball' style led him to be offered a coaching position at London Irish and then Bath. He coached England under-21s before being appointed the first ever full-time England coach in 1997. Woodward built up a formidable England squad, and his charges famously became the first team from the Northern hemisphere to lift the coveted Webb Ellis trophy in 2003. Woodward's overall record as England coach between 1997 and 2004 was an extremely impressive one: played 83, won 59, lost 22 and drawn 2. He was awarded a knighthood in the New Year's Honours in 2004.

*Clive Woodward
celebrates England's
World Cup win*

Sir Clive Ronald Woodward Factfile
Born: 6 Jan 1956 in Ely, Cambridgeshire
Clubs: Harlequins, Leicester, Manly (Australia)
Caps: 21 (W12, D2, L7)
Scoring: 4 tries – 16 pts
England debut: 19 Jan 1980 vs Ireland (Twickenham)

— BACK'S FORWARD THINKING —

Livewire openside flanker Neil Back may have an inappropriate name for a forward, but he holds the unique distinction of being the only England pack member ever to have dropped a goal in a test match. The Leicester number seven took his opportunity during his country's first ever visit to the Stadio Flaminio in Rome on 18 March 2000 in the inaugural Six Nations Championship. His 32nd minute short-range effort increased England's lead to 16–7 before they eventually went on to win the match 59–12.

However, five different forwards have dropped goals *against* England in an international: Charles Cathcart for Scotland at the Oval on 5 February 1872; John Boswell for Scotland at Leeds on 4 March 1893; Edmund Forrest, Ireland's captain, against England at Blackheath on 3 February 1894; Zinzan Brooke for New Zealand in the World Cup semi-final match in Cape Town on 18 June 1995; whilst Jean Prat, the great French flanker, scored four drop goals in three matches against England between 1951 and 1955.

— THE IRON MEN —

Will Carling holds the record for the most consecutive appearances for England, with 44 from 1989 to 1995. The top five reads:

Caps	Name	From	To
44	Will Carling	4 Nov 1989	4 Jun 1995
40	Jason Leonard	28 Jul 1990#	31 May 1995
36	John Pullin	20 Jan 1968	18 Jan 1975
33	Bill Beaumont	24 May 1975	16 Jan 1982*
30	Rory Underwood	14 Nov 1992	16 Mar 1996*

debut * final test of career

Carling was captain in all his matches in this sequence, while Beaumont, Pullin and Underwood played in every minute of every match during their unbroken spell in the team.

— ARGY BARGY —

England were due to tour Argentina in the summer of 1973 but were forced to cancel after Peronist groups threatened to kidnap the players. A hastily arranged short tour to Fiji and New Zealand was undertaken instead, which obviously caught the All Blacks on the hop as England gained an unlikely first victory on New Zealand soil in the only test at Eden Park.

— CHANGING TRY VALUES —

The value of a try has gradually increased over the years from zero (in the days when games were decided by the number of goals rather than points), up to the modern day value of five, first introduced in season 1992–93.

The following table lists the England player who had the honour of scoring his country's first try at the new try value, and the last try scored using an old value.

Value scorer	Date	First try scorer	Date	Last try
0 points	27 Mar 1871	Reginald Birkett	5 Mar 1887	George Jeffery
1 point	16 Feb 1889	Harry Bedford	7 Mar 1891	Dicky Lockwood
2 point	1 Mar 1890	Frank Evershed	4 Feb 1893	Ernest Taylor
3 point	6 Jan 1894	Samuel Morfitt	17 Apr 1971	Bob Hiller
4 point	12 Feb 1972	Chris Ralston	7 Mar 1992	Wade Dooley
5 point	17 Oct 1992	Ian Hunter		

— FIFTH DAY OF THE TEST! —

Originally, matches at Rugby School could last up to five days, with the captains asking the referee to set the length of the contest as required. The first international in 1871, England v Scotland, was 50 minutes each way, with the first mention of two 40 minute halves not finding their way into the Laws until 1926.

— PENALTIES GALORE —

In the early days of rugby, although some acts were deemed "unlawful" no specific penalty was demanded and usually the offence was followed by a scrummage. However, by 1882 a penalty kick was introduced for offside, although no goal could be dropped or placed from it.

It wasn't until 1888 that the RFU decided that a goal could be scored from a penalty, and by 1891 the International Board had accepted this as the norm.

The most penalty goals in an England international match:

For England:	Opponent (Venue)	Date	Result
8 Jonny Wilkinson	South Africa (Bloemfontein)*	24 Jun 2000	Won 27–22
7 Simon Hodgkinson	Wales (Cardiff)	19 Jan 1991	Won 25–6
7 Rob Andrew	Scotland (Twickenham)	18 Mar 1995	Won 24–12
7 Jonny Wilkinson	France (Twickenham)	20 Mar 1999	Won 21–10
7 Jonny Wilkinson	Fiji (Twickenham)	20 Oct 1999	Won 45–24
7 Jonny Wilkinson	South Africa (Twickenham)	24 Nov 2001	Won 29–9

Against:	Team (Venue)	Date	Result
6 Kieran Crowley**	for New Zealand (Christchurch)	1 Jun 1985	Lost 13–18
6 Michael Lynagh	for Australia (Brisbane)	29 May 1988	Lost 16–22
6 Gonzalo Quesada	for Argentina (Twickenham)	14 Dec 1996	Won 20–18
6 Neil Jenkins	for Wales (Wembley)	11 Apr 1999	Lost 31–32
6 Braam van Straaten	for South Africa (Pretoria)	17 Jun 2000	Lost 13–18
6 Gonzalo Quesada	for Argentina (Buenos Aires)	22 Jun 2002	Won 26–18
6 Dimitri Yachvili	for France (Twickenham)	13 Feb 2005	Lost 17–18

*A world rugby record 13 penalty goals were kicked in this match, eight by Wilkinson, four by Braam van Straaten and one by Percy Montgomery. In addition Wilkinson and van Straaten each missed an attempt at a penalty goal.
**On test debut

— SIX NATIONS RECORD —

Summary of England performances in the annual International Championship, nowadays known as the Six Nations Championship:

Outright Titles	25	(1883, 1884, 1892, 1910, 1913, 1914, 1921, 1923, 1924, 1928, 1930, 1934, 1937, 1953, 1957, 1958, 1963, 1980, 1991, 1992, 1995, 1996, 2000, 2001, 2003)
Shared Titles	10	(1886, 1890, 1912, 1920, 1932, 1939, 1947, 1954, 1960, 1973)
Grand Slams	12	(1913, 1914, 1921, 1923, 1924, 1928, 1957, 1980, 1991, 1992, 1995, 2003)
Triple Crowns	23	(1883, 1884, 1892, 1913, 1914, 1921, 1923, 1924, 1928, 1934, 1937, 1954, 1957, 1960, 1980, 1991, 1992, 1995, 1996, 1997, 1998, 2002, 2003)
Top points scorer	479	Jonny Wilkinson (1998–2008)
Top try scorer	18	Cyril Lowe (1913–23) and Rory Underwood (1984–96)
Most appearances	54	Jason Leonard (1991–2004)

— GREENWOOD SQUASHED —

Dick Greenwood, the England captain, missed the game with France at Twickenham on 22 February 1969 because he was hit in the eye by an opponent's racquet during a game of squash the night before the clash. Bedford forward Budge Rogers was handed the captaincy. The unlucky Greenwood never played for England again.

— JONNY 27 SOUTH AFRICA 22 —

Jonny Wilkinson's majestic 27 points against South Africa at Bloemfontein on 24 June 2000 meant the swashbuckling fly-half had contributed the entire points tally for the team, the highest England score with all the points being scored by the same player. Jonny landed eight penalty goals from nine attempts, plus a drop goal, in a 27–22 victory where he truly could have claimed he beat the Springboks on his own. The same cannot be said for Dusty Hare who scored all of England's 19 points against Wales at Twickenham in January 1981 – England still lost the match 21–19.

Opposite is the full list of matches where England's entire points tally has been scored by one player:

For England:	Date	Opponent (Venue)	Result
Jonny Wilkinson	24 Jun 2000	South Africa (Bloemfontein)	Won 27–22
Rob Andrew	18 Mar 1995	Scotland (Twickenham)	Won 24–12
Rob Andrew	27 May 1995	Argentina (Durban)	Won 24–18
Jonny Wilkinson	16 Nov 2003	France (Sydney)	Won 24–7
Rob Andrew	18 Jan 1986	Wales (Twickenham)	Won 21–18
Jonny Wilkinson	20 Mar 1999	France (Twickenham)	Won 21–10
Jonny Wilkinson	10 Nov 2001	Australia (Twickenham)	Won 21–15
Dusty Hare	17 Jan 1981	Wales (Twickenham)	Lost 19–21

And a list of matches where opposing players have monopolised their team's scoring against England:

Against:	Date	Team (Venue)	Result
Matt Burke	18 Nov 2000	for Australia (Twickenham)	Won 22–19
Duncan Hodge	2 Apr 2000	for Scotland (Murrayfield)	Lost 13–19
Kieran Crowley*	1 Jun 1985	for New Zealand (Christchurch)	Lost 13–18
Gonzalo Quesada	14 Dec 1996	for Argentina (Twickenham)	Won 20–18
Braam van Straaten	17 Jun 2000	for South Africa (Pretoria)	Lost 13–18
Gonzalo Quesada	22 Jun 2002	for Argentina (Buenos Aires)	Won 26–18
Dimitri Yachvili	13 Feb 2005	for France (Twickenham)	Lost 17–18

*On test debut

— ENGLAND LEGENDS: MARTIN JOHNSON —

"We did it!"

When he held aloft the William Webb Ellis Cup in Sydney on 22 November 2003, Martin Johnson became the first Englishman to skipper his country to a World Cup triumph. Victory over Australia in a tense final capped a superb year for Johnson, who had previously led the England team to a Grand Slam in the 2003 Six Nations Championship – their first success in the expanded competition and a first Slam since 1995.

Johnson's international career began when he played for the England 18-Group in 1987. His senior England debut came as a late replacement for Wade Dooley in 1993, and later that year he toured New Zealand with the British Lions, again replacing Dooley. Altogether, Johnson competed in ten Five/Six Nations tournaments and also played in the World Cups of 1995 and in 1999, taking over the captaincy in the latter event.

His leadership qualities earned him the captaincy of the British Lions and he became the only man to skipper the Lions on two separate tours, to South Africa in 1997 and Australia 2001.

With his club, Leicester, Johnson experienced yet more success. He led the Tigers to a Pilkington Cup victory in 1997, four successive Premiership titles between 1999 and 2002, and back-to-back European Cup triumphs in 2001 and 2002.

On 1 July 2008 Johnson became Team Manager of England, replacing Brian Ashton.

Martin Osborne Johnson CBE Factfile
Born: 9 Mar 1970 in Solihull, Warwickshire
Clubs: Wigston, Tihoi (NZ), College Old Boys (NZ), King
Country (NZ), Leicester
Caps: 84 (W67, D2, L15)
Scoring: 2 tries – 10 pts
England debut: 16 Jan 1993 vs France (Twickenham)

— FULL HOUSE —

Only five players have scored for England by all four methods (try,
conversion, penalty goal, drop goal) in a single match, Jonny
Wilkinson being the only one to achieve the feat twice.

For England:	Date	Opponent (Venue)	Result
Rob Andrew	4 Jun 1994	South Africa (Pretoria)	Won 32–15
Paul Grayson	22 Mar 1998	Scotland (Murrayfield)	Won 34–20
Jonny Wilkinson	23 Mar 2002	Wales (Twickenham)	Won 50–10
Jonny Wilkinson	9 Nov 2002	New Zealand (Twickenham)	Won 31–28
Charlie Hodgson	20 Nov 2004	South Africa (Twickenham)	Won 32–16
Against:	**Date**	**Team (Venue)**	**Result**
Jerry Shea	17 Jan 1920	for Wales (Swansea)	Lost 5–19
Don Clarke	25 May 1963	for New Zealand (Auckland)	Lost 11–21
Jean-Pierre Romeu	2 Mar 1974	for France (Paris)	Drew 12–12
Christophe Lamaison	1 Mar 1997	for France (Twickenham)	Lost 20–23
James Hook	17 Mar 2007	for Wales (Cardiff)	Lost 18–27

— WILLIAM WEBB ELLIS TROPHY —

The William Webb Ellis Trophy is the prize presented to the winners of the Rugby World Cup. The cup itself was made in 1906 and was subsequently chosen as an appropriate trophy for use in the World Cup competition. The words 'International Rugby Board' and, below, 'William Webb Ellis Cup' are engraved on the face of the trophy. The cup, which is often referred to simply as the Rugby World Cup, stands at 38 centimetres and is silver gilded in gold. It is supported by two cast scroll handles, one having the head of a satyr and the other the head of a nymph.

World Cup winners
1987 New Zealand
1991 Australia
1995 South Africa
1999 Australia
2003 England
2007 South Africa

— FRIMLEY FLY-HALVES —

England team mates Jonny Wilkinson and Toby Flood were both born in the small Surrey town of Frimley (population just 12,739 at the 2001 census). Not only that, but both births were six years apart in the same ward of the local maternity hospital.

— CONVERSIONS —

In the early days what we know now as a conversion was known as a "try for goal", which is where the modern term "try" actually comes from (because scoring one gave you a "try" at scoring a goal).

Up until the 1958/59 season the kick at goal after a try had to be taken accompanied by a "placer", a person who lay on the ground and held the ball for the kicker to make the attempt.

Here are the most conversions scored in an international for and against England:

For England:	Opponent (Venue)	Date	Result
15 Paul Grayson	v Netherlands (Huddersfield)	14 Nov 1998	Won 110–0
14 Charlie Hodgson*	v Romania (Twickenham)	17 Nov 2001	Won 134–0
13 Jonny Wilkinson	v United States (Twickenham)	21 Aug 1999	Won 106–8
12 Paul Grayson	v Tonga (Twickenham)	15 Oct 1999	Won 101–10
11 Paul Grayson	v Uruguay (Brisbane)	2 Nov 2003	Won 111–13

Against:	Team (Venue)	Date	Result
7 Percy Montgomery	for South Africa (Bloemfontein)	26 May 2007	Lost 10–58
5 John Allan	for Scotland (Murrayfield)	21 Mar 1931	Lost 19–28
5 Keith Jarrett*	for Wales (Cardiff)	15 Apr 1967	Lost 21–34
5 Pierre Villepreux	for President's XV (Twickenham)	17 Apr 1971	Lost 11–28
5 Pierre Villepreux	for France (Paris)	26 Feb 1972	Lost 12–37
5 Andrew Mehrtens	for New Zealand (Dunedin)	20 Jun 1998	Lost 22–64
5 Stirling Mortlock	for Australia (Melbourne)	17 Jun 2006	Lost 18–43

*On test debut

— OJO JOINS MAGNIFICENT SEVEN —

Topsy Ojo scored two tries on his England test debut against New Zealand in Auckland on 14 June 2008, joining a select band of just seven players to have scored a brace of tries for any country against the All Blacks on test debut. Only two other Englishmen appear in the list, the legendary Alexander Obolensky at Twickenham in 1936 and Harlequins centre Robert Lloyd also at Twickenham in 1967.

— ENGLAND LEGENDS: JONNY WILKINSON —

Jonny racks up some of his 1,032 pts for England

Points machine Jonny Wilkinson will always be remembered as the man who dropped the winning goal at the 2003 Rugby World Cup final in Sydney, but as a player Wilkinson is much more than that.

A totally dedicated individual who practices incessantly, Jonny burst on to the scene as a precocious 18 year old talent and has gone on to gain 70 caps in a 10 year test career during which time he has accumulated a world record 1,032 points for England. With his five British & Irish Lions caps and 67 points for them he has accumulated 1,099 test points.

Despite long injury and frustrating layoffs between the 2003 and 2007 Rugby World Cups Wilkinson returned in a somewhat talismanic role to lead England to the brink of retaining the Webb Elis Trophy in Paris.

Jonathan Peter Wilkinson MBE Factfile
Born: 25 May 1979 in Frimley, Surrey
Clubs: Newcastle Falcons
Caps: 70 (W53, L17)
Scoring: 6T, 144C, 209PG, 29DG – 1,032 pts
England debut: 4 Apr 1998 vs Ireland (Twickenham)

— THE EARLY BATH —

In the fourth minute of the second test against Australia at Ballymore on 31 May 1975, Mike Burton became the first England player ever to be sent off. Australian referee Bob Burnett gave Burton his marching orders for a late charge on wing Douglas Osborne after he had kicked ahead.

The only time an England player and an opponent have been dismissed at the same time was when Lewis Moody and Alesana Tuilagi had an altercation during the England-Samoa test at Twickenham on 26 November 2005. The two were Leicester Tigers club teammates at the time!

Interestingly, whilst just four England players have been sent off the ignominy of the early bath has been bestowed on eleven opponents.

Sent Off

For England:	Opponent (**Venue**)	Date	Referee
Mike Burton	v Australia (Brisbane)	31 May 1975	Bob Burnett
Danny Grewcock	v New Zealand (Dunedin)	20 Jun 1998	Wayne Erickson
Simon Shaw	v New Zealand (Auckland)	19 Jun 2004	Nigel Williams
Lewis Moody	v Samoa (Twickenham)	26 Nov 2005	Mark Lawrence

Against:	Team (**Venue**)	Date	Referee
Cyril Brownlie	for New Zealand (Twickenham)	3 Jan 1925	Albert Freethy
Paul Ringer	for Wales (Twickenham)	16 Feb 1980	David Burnett
Noa Nadruku	for Fiji (Twickenham)	4 Nov 1989	Brian Stirling
Tevita Vonolagi	for Fiji (Twickenham)	4 Nov 1989	Brian Stirling
Federico Mendez	for Argentina (Twickenham)	3 Nov 1990	Colin Hawke
Gregoire Lascube	for France (Paris)	15 Feb 1992	Stephen Hilditch

Vincent Moscato	for France (Paris)	15 Feb 1992	Stephen Hilditch
John Davies	for Wales (Cardiff)	18 Feb 1995	Didier Mene
Ngalu Taufo'ou	for Tonga (Twickenham)	15 Oct 1999	Wayne Erickson
Jannes Labuschagne	for S Africa (Twickenham)	23 Nov 2002	Paddy O'Brien
Alesana Tuilagi	for Samoa (Twickenham)	26 Nov 2005	Mark Lawrence

— SECOND HALF ZEROS —

The biggest half-time lead England has conceded to then lose a match is 11 points. On 13 February 2005 England lead France at Twickenham 17–6 at the break, but the visitors went on to win the game 18–17.

— ENGLISH ROSE —

Prior to the English team being dispatched to Edinburgh to play a Scottish side for the first ever international match in 1871, the Rugby Football Union chose a red rose as the side's emblem, and subsequently England have worn a red rose on their shirts in every one of their 580 international matches.

The flower was chosen in reverence to the Tudor Rose, a traditional English emblem symbolising the end of the War of the Roses in 1485. It is, however, almost certainly no coincidence that a red rose also appears in the crest of Rugby School after its founder, Lawrence Sheriff, was granted a coat of arms featuring the Tudor Rose by Elizabeth I.

Over the years the red rose appeared on the white shirt of England in various forms, shapes and sizes. For instance, in a photograph of the England team taken at Twickenham on 25 January 1913, all players have different versions of a red rose. In the one on the shirt of Cherry Pillman, the stalk of his flower is pointing in a different direction to the others. The fashion for swapping jerseys with an opponent following a game had not yet taken root, so it seems that many England players would have worn the same jersey for the duration of their careers, and as new players were introduced to the team they would have had their roses embroidered individually and in isolation, hence the disparities in design.

However, in 1920, Alfred Wright, an employee of the Rugby Football Union, created a uniform design for the now famous emblem which was used on England jerseys, virtually without alteration, until the 1998/99 season. When Nike replaced Cotton Traders as the RFU's official kit supplier, they introduced the modern version of the England Rugby 'Red Rose' that adorns the modern England shirt and, indeed, the cover of this book.

— THE CENTURY MAKERS —

One Hundred Points for England:

	Player	Career	Tries	Conv	Pens	Drops	Points	Caps
1	Jonny Wilkinson	1998–2008	6	144	209	29	1032	66+4
2	Paul Grayson	1995–2004	2	78	72	6	400	24+8
3	Rob Andrew	1985–1997	2	33	86	21	396	69+2
4	Jon Webb	1987–1993	4	41	66	-	296	32+1
5	Charlie Hodgson	2001–2008	6	44	44	3	259	25+5
6	Dusty Hare	1974–1984	2	14	67	1	240	25
7	Rory Underwood	1984–1996	49	-	-	-	210	85
8	Simon Hodgkinson	1989–1991	1	35	43	-	203	14
9=	Will Greenwood	1997–2005	31	-	-	-	155	55
9=	Ben Cohen	2000–2006	31	-	-	-	155	54+3
11	Jerry Guscott	1989–1999	30	-	-	2	143	62+3
12	Mike Catt	1994–2007	7	16	22	3	142	62+13
13	Jason Robinson	2001–2007	28	-	-	-	140	47+4
14	Bob Hiller	1968–1972	3	12	33	2	138	19
15	Dan Luger	1998–2003	24	-	-	-	120	32+6
16	Josh Lewsey	1998–2007	22	-	-	-	110	53+2
17	Matt Dawson	1995–2006	16	6	3	-	101	55+22

— IT'S A NUMBERS GAME —

Photographic evidence supports the fact that England wore numbers on the backs of their white shirts for the first time against Wales at Cardiff Arms Park on 21 January 1922. However, the following year against France at Stade Colombes England did not wear numbers. Numbers have been a regular feature on England shirts since the mid 1920s, although for many years they did not match today's numbering sequence.

Up until 1961 the full-back wore '1' with the rest of the backs following on up to '7', the pack wore numbers 8 to 15. The modern numbering system was first adopted for the visit of the Springboks to Twickenham on 7 January 1961.

England have worn numbers on their shorts for only 11 matches in their history, during both the 1995 and 1999 Rugby World Cup competitions.

— ENGLAND LEGENDS: RICHARD SHARP —

Richard Sharp stormed onto the international stage in January 1960 with an imperious debut performance at fly-half against Wales. His rapid elevation to test colours was even more remarkable in that he stepped up for the injured Bev Risman at the last possible moment, so late in fact that he was not even listed in the match programme. Sharp was considered a vital cog in the side which took the 1960 Triple Crown, and led the team when England won the Five Nations championship three years later.

Sharp, who was born in India and came to England when he was aged eight, was schooled at Blundell's in Devon and eventually became a commando in the Royal Marines. Following his retirement from rugby he became a journalist, covering rugby for *The Sunday Telegraph*. He was awarded the OBE in 1986.

Richard Adrian William Sharp OBE Factfile
Born: 9 Sep 1938 in Mysore, India
Clubs: Redruth, Wasps, Bristol
Caps: 14 (W7, D4, L3)
Scoring: 2T, 4C, 1PG, 3DG – 26 pts
England debut: 16 Jan 1960 vs Wales (Twickenham)

*Sixties sensation
Richard Sharp*

— BARREN SPELLS —

Players who have made the most test match appearances without scoring a single try:

Games	Name	From	To	Notes	Tryless mins
63	Jason Leonard	1 Feb 1997	15 Feb 2004*	Last 63 games	4075
54	Graham Rowntree	18 Mar 1995	17 Jun 2006	Entire career	3510
50	Jason Leonard	28 Jul 1990#	23 Nov 1996	First 50 games	4049
49	Brian Moore	4 Mar 1989	22 Jun 1995*	Last 49 games	3865
43	Danny Grewcock	29 Nov 1997	15 Feb 2004		2248
41	Peter Wheeler	1 Feb 1975	17 Mar 1984	Entire career	3244
37	Martin Johnson	28 Aug 1999	22 Nov 2003*	Last 37 games	2822
36	Rob Andrew	5 Jan 1985#	16 Mar 1991	First 36 games	2883
36	Gary Pearce	3 Feb 1979	11 Oct 1991	Entire career	2880

Debut   * Last game

— THEY SAID IT —

"Rugby must always be amateur, which means playing in one's spare time for recreation. If a man wants to play professional rugby, good luck to him. But there's no room for him in our game."
Wavell Wakefield, former England captain and RFU president

"Never mind, you had the nicest jerseys."
Welsh supporter to the chairman of the England selectors after Wales's 27–3 win in 1979

"It was like MASH in the medical room."
Leon Walkden, RFU doctor, after the violent England v Wales game in 1980

"I prefer rugby to soccer . . . I enjoy the violence in rugby, except when they start biting each other's ears off."
Elizabeth Taylor, film star, 1972

"Handling the ball is only a minor part of your job, so don't give much thought to it."
Dai Gent, ex-England international, writing about forward play in his book *Rugby Football* in 1933

"When in doubt, decide against the side making the most noise. They are probably in the wrong."
Scottish umpire **H.H. Almond** after awarding his country a hotly disputed try against England in the very first international match in 1871

"This is a rugby match, not a cattle sale."
The SRU president **Mr James Aitken Smith** at Twickenham in 1928 to King George V after the monarch had asked why the Scots were not wearing numbers

"The only place for a coach in rugby is for transporting the teams to the match."
England captain **Eric Evans** in 1957

"In the mid eighties, selection for England was the modern equivalent of being named as accredited food taster for Attila the Hun."
Rob Andrew in his autobiography *A Game and a Half*

"Being dropped by England and Take That splitting up on the same day is enough to finish anyone off."
Martin Bayfield, the England lock, after being dropped in 1994

"I thought I would have a quiet pint, followed by about 17 noisy ones."
England prop **"Coochie" Chilcott** on his retirement day plans

"We tried to handle the ball in the wrong places, and I blame the media for that."
England coach **Jack Rowell** at the 1995 World Cup in South Africa

— THREE IN LEEDS —

England have played three home matches in the city of Leeds, all at different grounds: in 1884 Cardigan Fields was used for the visit of Wales (won by 1 goal and 2 tries to a goal); nine years later Headingley was the venue when Scotland (lost 0–8) were the opposition; and in 1896 Meanwood Road (lost 4–10) hosted Ireland.

— FOUR FORENAMES —

Two England internationals have had four first names:

Quentin Eric Moffitt Ayres KING
Arthur Fairfax Charles Coryndon LUXMOORE

— 'ER' INDOORS —

England have played five internationals under a closed roof:

Date	Venue	Opponents	Result
21 Jun 2003	Telstra Dome, Melbourne	v Australia	Won 25–14
26 Oct 2003	Telstra Dome, Melbourne	v Samoa	Won 35–22
5 Feb 2005	Millennium Stadium, Cardiff	v Wales	Lost 9–11
17 Jun 2006	Telstra Dome, Melbourne	v Australia	Lost 18–43
17 Mar 2007	Millennium Stadium, Cardiff	v Wales	Lost 18–27

— HOME AND AWAY AT WEMBLEY —

Wembley Stadium holds the unique distinction in English rugby history of having hosted both an England home test match and an away one.

On 17 October 1992 England entertained Canada in the first rugby union international match to be staged at the home of English football – predictably England ran out 26–13 victors.

Six years later Wembley was once more the venue for an England game. On this occasion, though, England were the visitors as Wales had temporarily moved their home games to the English capital whilst the new Millennium Stadium in Cardiff was being built on the site of the old National Stadium. Despite playing on 'home' soil, it proved to be a day England would rather forget as a chance to claim their 12th Grand Slam spectacularly backfired against an inspired Welsh side. Wales won the match 32–31 after Neil Jenkins calmly slotted over an 83rd minute conversion of Scott Gibbs' last-gasp try.

Many years earlier, England first played rugby union at the famous old ground on 14 April 1942 when they lost 5–8 to Scotland in a wartime Services international for which no caps were awarded.

— DORIS IS JONNY'S KEY —

In June 1998 when Jonny Wilkinson was preparing for his first test in the No 10 jersey against the Wallabies in Brisbane, and his first game as England's frontline goalkicker, he was having serious problems with his kicking technique. Despite hours of training with England kicking coach Dave Alred, Wilko was becoming increasingly frustrated as he sprayed his kicks well wide of the goals.

Finally, Alred said to him: "Forget the posts, let's aim for something else. Imagine there's a woman sitting in that seat, 20 rows back behind the posts. Let's aim for her."

Wilkinson himself recalled in *The Times* in 2003: "She became known as Doris – we picked out a seat for her and tried to hit her."

As Wilkinson's kicking improved, the pair imagined an ice-cream in Doris's hand which Jonny had to hit; then, finally, Alred nominated the ultimate target: a chocolate flake in the ice-cream in Doris's hand. From that day, whenever his kicking practice has been poor, it has been Wilkinson's habit to change his approach and "hit a few Dorises"!

— WORLD CUP WIN IN STATS —

RUGBY WORLD CUP FINAL 2003
22 November, Stadium Australia, Sydney

England	v	Australia
Josh Lewsey	15	Mat Rogers
Jason Robinson	14	Wendell Sailor
Will Greenwood	13	Stirling Mortlock
Mike Tindall	12	Elton Flatley
Ben Cohen	11	Lote Tuqiri
Jonny Wilkinson	10	Steve Larkham
Matt Dawson	9	George Gregan (capt)
Trevor Woodman	1	Bill Young
Steve Thompson	2	Brendan Cannon
Phil Vickery	3	Alastair Baxter
Martin Johnson (capt)	4	Justin Harrison
Ben Kay	5	Nathan Sharpe
Richard Hill	6	George Smith
Lawrence Dallaglio	7	David Lyons
Neil Back	8	Phil Waugh

Bench:

Dorian West	16
Jason Leonard	17
Martin Corry	18
Lewis Moody	19
Kyran Bracken	20
Mike Catt	21
Iain Balshaw	22

Replacements used:
Catt for Tindall 78
Leonard for Vickery 81
Balshaw for Lewsey 85
Moody for Hill 93

Bench:
Jeremy Paul
Matt Dunning
David Giffin
Matt Cockbain
Chris Whitaker
Matt Giteau
Joe Roff

Replacements used:
Giteau for Larkham 18–30
Giteau for Larkham 55–63
Paul for Cannon 56
Cockbain for Lyons 56
Roff for Sailor 70
Giteau for Larkham 85
Dunning for Young 92

Scoring sequence:

		E-A
06 mins:	Tuqiri (Try)	0–5
10 mins:	Wilkinson (PG)	3–5
18 mins:	Wilkinson (PG)	6–5
27 mins:	Wilkinson (PG)	9–5
38 mins:	Robinson (Try)	14–5
47 mins:	Flatley (PG)	14–8
60 mins:	Flatley (PG)	14–11
79 mins:	Flatley (PG)	14–14
82 mins:	Wilkinson (PG)	17–14
97 mins:	Flatley (PG)	17–17
99 mins:	Wilkinson (DG)	20–17

Referee: Andre Watson (South Africa).
Attendance: 82,957.

— ENGLAND LEGENDS: JEREMY GUSCOTT —

Jeremy Guscott marked his international debut against Romania in 1989 by becoming the first England player for 82 years to score a hat-trick of tries on his test bow. He went on to become one of only three players to have scored tries in each of their first four England appearances. An ever-present member of the England team which won Five Nations Grand Slams in 1991, 1992 and 1995, Guscott also featured in three World Cup squads, collecting a runners' up medal in 1991.

Guscott scored his final two international tries in his last game against Tonga taking his tally to 30 tries, leaving him second in England's all-time list behind wing Rory Underwood.

At club level, he made his debut for Bath in 1984. He continued playing for the Somerset outfit during the final years of the amateur era when they were a major force in English rugby. His medal haul throughout this period was an impressive one, consisting of six league titles, six domestic cup winners medals and a European Cup winners medal.

Jeremy Clayton Guscott MBE Factfile
Born: 7 Jul 1965 in Bath, Somerset
Club: Bath
Caps: 65 (W51, L14)
Scoring: 30T, 2DG – 143 pts
England debut: 13 Mar 1989 vs Romania (Bucharest)

— BATH: ALMOST HALF FULL —

When England played South Africa in Cape Town on 11 June 1994 Jack Rowell, the former Bath supremo, named five of his former charges in the team: Phil de Glanville, Victor Ubogu, Nigel Redman, Steve Ojomoh and Ben Clarke. In addition, he named five more Bath players on the replacements bench – Mike Catt, Stuart Barnes, John Mallett, Graham Dawe and Adedayo Adebayo – although none of this quintet made it onto the field. Nonetheless, the total of ten players (out of 21 on duty) from one club set a new England record.

— SCHOOL CAPS —

Three players have been capped for England while still at school:

Player	School	Match	Date
Ryder Richardson	Manchester Grammar School	v Ireland (Manchester)	5 Feb 1881
Frank Wright	Edinburgh Academy	v Scotland (Edinburgh)	19 Mar 1881
Jumbo Milton	Bedford School	v Wales (Leicester)	9 Jan 1904

— THE LONG AND THE SHORT OF IT —

Froude "Baby" Hancock of Blackheath and Somerset, who won three England caps in the pack between 1886 and 1890, was the first true giant to wear his country colours. In 1891, when he toured South Africa with the British Lions, he stood at 6 ft 5 ins (1.95m) and weighed a massive 17st 2lb (108kg). By 1896, when he again toured the Republic with the Lions, Hancock was even bigger, having put on an extra 20lbs. A newspaper report of the time described him as "the king of the lineout, but a real problem to fit into a scrum". During his career he travelled from Somerset to London every week to play for Blackheath, often having to walk the final ten miles of his journey home.

One of the shortest players to win an England cap was John King, a forward who gained 12 caps between 1911–13 and was just 5ft 5 ins tall. The tallest England player is lock Martin Bayfield (31 caps, 1991–96), who stood at 6 ft 10 ins (2.08m). Bayfield's outsized frame later earned him an unlikely role as Robbie Coltrane's body double in the Harry Potter films.

— BEDOUIN MEN —

Two England players have won England caps with four different clubs:

Lock forward Mike Davis won 16 caps between 1963–70. He began his international career with Torquay Athletic (10 caps), before being capped with Devonport Services against Wales in 1966. Davis then won his 12th cap against Australia the following January while playing for United Services before finishing his England career at Harlequins (4 caps).

Rob Andrew won his first nine England caps between 1985 and

1986 while at Nottingham. He switched to Wasps with whom he won the lion's share of his caps, before continuing his England career at Toulouse in 1992. Andrew was awarded his final cap against Wales in March 1997 while director of rugby at Newcastle Falcons.

— A THREE NATIONS CHAMPIONSHIP —

The formation of the International Rugby Board in 1886 can be traced back to a controversial encounter between England and Scotland at the Rectory Field Blackheath on 1 March 1884. The Scots hotly disputed England's try, scored by Richard Kindersley, arguing that there had been a knock back on their side. After a ten-minute heated discussion the Irish referee, Mr G Scriven, ruled that the infringement would have given England the advantage anyway, dismissed the Scots' appeal and awarded a conversion near the posts. Wilfred Bolton duly slotted his kick to give England victory by a goal to a try.

The argument between the two countries rumbled on leading to the cancellation of the 1885 fixture. Then, when the other Home Unions decided to form an International Rugby Board at a meeting in Manchester the following year, England refused to be bound by it. Consequently, England did not play any matches in either the 1888 or 1889 Championships which, for the only time, became Three Nations affairs. England eventually joined the international body in April 1890.

— FOUR IN A ROW —

Just two players have scored four successive tries for England without any of their team-mates also crossing the line in between. The first to accomplish this rare feat was Cyril Lowe in 1914. He scored England's final try against Ireland in a 17–12 win and then continued his scoring spree with the first three tries in England's next test against Scotland in Inverleith.

In more recent times, Ben Cohen equalled Lowe's achievement in three games during England's autumn internationals at Twickenham in 2002. After scoring England's last try in their 31–28 victory over New Zealand, he maintained his scoring form with his side's only two five pointers against Australia in a 32–31 win. For good measure, Cohen then notched England's first try in the 53–3 demolition of the Springboks at Twickenham in November 2002.

— FAVOURITE FOES —

England's top performers against individual countries:

Opponent	Most matches	Most points	Most tries
Argentina	6 Jason Leonard	49 Simon Hodgkinson	3 Rory Underwood
Australia	12 Mike Catt	102 Jonny Wilkinson	4 Rory Underwood/ Ben Cohen
Fiji	3 by five players	32 Rory Underwood	8 Rory Underwood
France	18 Jason Leonard	153 Jonny Wilkinson	8 Daniel Lambert
Ireland	14 Rory Underwood	86 Jonny Wilkinson	7 Rory Underwood
Italy	9 Leonard/Dawson	130 Jonny Wilkinson	6 Austin Healey
New Zealand	8 Matt Dawson	47 Jonny Wilkinson	2 by nine players
Scotland	14 Jason Leonard	91 Jonny Wilkinson	6 Cyril Lowe/ Jason Robinson
South Africa	12 Jason Leonard	127 Jonny Wilkinson	4 Will Greenwood
Wales	14 Rory Underwood	151 Jonny Wilkinson	7 Will Greenwood

Martin Johnson was never on the losing side in nine matches against Scotland, Jason Leonard and Matt Dawson never lost in nine appearances against Italy, whilst Ben Cohen won all his seven games versus Wales. Nigel Horton, the Moseley lock, lost all his five games against Wales.

— SLAM DUNK! —

The games that clinched England's dozen Grand Slams:

15 March 1913   vs Scotland at Twickenham (won 3–0)
13 April 1914   vs France at Stade Colombes, Paris (won 39–13)
28 March 1921   vs France at Stade Colombes, Paris (won 10–6)
2 April 1923   vs France at Stade Colombes, Paris (won 12–3)
15 April 1924   vs Scotland at Twickenham (won 19–0)
17 March 1928   vs Scotland at Twickenham (won 6–0)
16 March 1957   vs Scotland at Twickenham (won 16–3)
15 March 1980   vs Scotland at Murrayfield (won 30–18)
16 March 1991   vs France at Twickenham (won 21–19)*
7 March 1992   vs Wales at Twickenham (won 24–0)
18 March 1995   vs Scotland at Twickenham (won 24–12)*
30 March 2003   vs Ireland at Lansdowne Road (won 42–6)*
* Grand Slam deciders between teams with 100% records before the match

— ANNIE, GET YOUR SON —

Rory and Tony Underwood hold the record for the most appearances together for England by a pair of brothers, playing in the same team on 19 occasions between 1992 and 1996.

The Underwoods were the eighth set of brothers to have appeared in the same England team, following a lineage originally established by Reginald and Louis Birkett who were included in the England XX against Scotland at Raeburn Place, Edinburgh on 8 March 1875.

One of the most enduring rugby images of the nineties was of Annie Underwood, Rory and Tony's mother, celebrating wildly in the stands at the Five Nations game against Scotland at Twickenham when Tony went over for a try in the 51st minute, just five minutes after elder brother Rory had also scored.

Apart from Mrs Underwood's boys, the only brothers to have scored tries in the same match for England were Percy and Franck Stout against Wales at Blackheath on 2 April 1898.

The Underwoods broke the existing record of ten appearances by brothers in the same England team – set by Temple and Charles Gurdon between 1880 and 1886 – on 12 November 1994 against Romania at Twickenham. The duo capped a memorable occasion by both scoring tries – Tony (2) and Rory (1) in a comprehensive 54–3 win.

— BAT AND BALL —

Albert 'Monkey' Hornby was the first player to represent England at both rugby and cricket. He made his rugby debut for England at the Oval on 5 February 1877 against Ireland, scoring a try, and then appeared in a cricket test at the same venue against Australia in August 1882, scoring 2 and 9 with the bat.

Dual Internationals	England Rugby	Test Cricket
"Monkey" Hornby	9 caps (1877–1892)	3 tests (1879–1884)
George Vernon	5 caps (1878–1881)	1 test (1882)
Andrew Stoddart	10 caps (1885–1893)	16 tests (1888–1898)
William Milton	2 caps (1874–1875)	3 tests for South Africa (1889–1892)
Frank Mitchell	6 caps (1895–1896)	2 tests for England (1899) & 3 for South Africa (1912)

Samuel Woods	13 caps (1890–1895)	3 tests for Australia (1888) & 3 for England (1895–1896)
Reggie Spooner	1 cap (1903)	10 tests (1905–1912)
Reggie Schwarz	3 caps (1899–1901)	20 tests for South Africa (1906–1912)
Reginald Hands	2 caps (1910)	1 test for South Africa (1914)
Tuppy Owen-Smith	10 caps (1934–1937)	5 tests (1929)
Martin Donnelly	1 cap (1947)	7 tests for New Zealand (1937–1949)
C.B. van Ryneveld	4 caps (1949)	19 tests for South Africa (1951–58)
M.J.K. Smith	1 cap (1956)	50 tests (1958–1972)

— UNION TO LEAGUE AND BACK AGAIN —

John Bentley began his unique career playing amateur rugby league for Dewsbury Moore before he joined Cleckheaton RUFC. He then played for Otley and Sale, with whom he won the first two of his England rugby union caps against Ireland and Australia in Brisbane in the spring of 1988.

However, in November 1988 Bentley signed professional rugby league forms in a reported £80,000 transfer to Leeds. In February 1992 he scored a try on his debut for Great Britain against France in Perpignan. After joining Halifax in August 1992, Bentley won his second Great Britain cap against France in Carcassonne in March 1994, before playing for England in the 1995 rugby league World Cup.

When rugby union turned professional in 1995 it paved a way back to the 15-man game for Bentley and he signed for Newcastle Falcons in September 1996, playing rugby league for Huddersfield in the summer as well. He was selected for the British Lions tour to South Africa in 1997, appearing in the second and third tests of a victorious series. After the tour, Bentley flew to Australia to play in the Cook Cup test against Australia at the Sydney Football Stadium, over nine years since winning his last rugby union cap for England. Bentley was capped for the last time against South Africa at Twickenham in November 1997 and eventually finished his union career at Rotherham.

— CHARIOT BEGINS ITS JOURNEY —

The singing of 'Swing Low, Sweet Chariot' by England supporters is a relatively recent phenomenon that reputedly began with England's extraordinary second-half performance against Ireland at Twickenham on 19 March 1988. Trailing 3–0 at the break, England responded by scoring 35 unanswered points during the second period. As the scoreboard ticked over, the crowd began singing the song which had been a popular rugby club ditty throughout the country for many years. Seven months later 'Swing Low, Sweet Chariot' rung out at Twickenham again when England beat the Wallabies 28–19 in Will Carling's first match as captain to cement the song's status as an unofficial English anthem.

— CHRISTMAS DAY BABIES —

A surprising fact is that the most popular day for England players to be born is in fact Christmas Day, with ten future internationals born on 25 December:

Charles Sherrard	1849	2 caps 1871–72
Thomas Blatherwick	1855	1 cap 1878
Bernard Middleton	1858	2 caps 1882–83
Maffer Davey	1880	2 caps 1908–09
Andrew Slocock	1886	8 caps 1907–08
John Wallens	1901	1 cap 1927
Harold Wheatley	1912	7 caps 1936–39
Nigel Starmer–Smith	1944	7 caps 1969–71
Kevin Simms	1964	15 caps 1985–88
Mark Mapletoft	1971	1 cap 1997

— SICK NOTE CAP —

Ernie Woodhead, a student at Trinity College, Dublin was asked to play for England against Ireland at Lansdowne Road on 30 January 1880 after several of the visiting team were laid low by seasickness during the crossing of the Irish Sea. Despite performing capably in the 0–0 draw, Woodhead was not called up by his country again.

— TV FIRST —

The England-Scotland game at Twickenham on 19 March 1938 was the first rugby international to be shown on television. BBC viewers enjoyed a thrilling match in which the lead changed hands on five occasions, Scotland eventually prevailing 21–16.

Eleven years earlier, the England-Wales game at Twickenham on 15 January 1927 was the first to be broadcast on radio. Teddy Wakelam, the former Harlequins back-rower, was the man with the mic as England recorded an 11–9 victory.

— NOT SO SMART —

On 20 February 1982 England travelled to Paris and beat France 27–15 at Parc des Princes. At the post-match banquet each player was presented with a bottle of expensive aftershave by their hosts. Spirits were high when Maurice Colclough, who had been playing his rugby for Angouleme in the French league at the time, sneakily emptied the contents of his gift into a nearby potted plant, replacing the sweet smelling liquid with white wine. He then got to his feet, downed the drink and dared anyone to follow his example. Never one to shirk a challenge, England prop Colin Smart promptly gulped down his bottle of aftershave in one. Known from that moment on as Colin 'Not-so' Smart, he was rushed to hospital but, happily, was well enough two weeks later to take his place against Wales.

— AT LEAST WE TURN UP —

The 1972 Five Nations Championship will always be remembered as the year that both Wales and Scotland refused to play in Dublin because of the escalating tensions in Northern Ireland in the wake of the tragic events of Bloody Sunday. Ireland's next home game in the Championship was scheduled for 10 February 1973 against England, but it was widely thought that this game would also fall a victim to 'The Troubles'. However, John Pullin led his England team out on to the Lansdowne Road turf to receive a resounding standing ovation. After his side suffered a 9–18 defeat, Pullin memorably commented: "We might not be much good, but at least we turn up."

— CODE BREAKERS —

UNION TO LEAGUE

Name	Union	England RL	GB RL
Robert Poole	1896	1903	-
George Marsden	1900	1905	-
Patsy Boylan	1908	-	1908
Alf Wood	1908	-	1911–1914
Thomas Woods	1908	-	1911
Tom Woods	1920–1921	Wales 1922	-
David Holland	1912	-	1914
Jim Brough	1925	-	1928–1936
Tom Danby	1949	-	1950
Bev Risman	1959–1961*		
		-	1968
Ray French	1961	-	1968
Mike Coulman	1967–1968*	-	1971
Keith Fielding	1969–1972	1975	1974–1977
Keith Smith	1974–1975	1979	-
Peter Williams	1987 (4 caps)	-	1989
John Bentley	1988–97*	1995–96	1992–94

LEAGUE TO UNION

Name	England RL	GB RL	Union
John Bentley	1995–96	1992–94	1988–97*
Barrie-Jon Mather	1995	1994–96	1999
Jason Robinson	1995–96	1997–99	2001–2007*
Henry Paul	NZ	-	2002–2004
Andy Farrell	1993–2004	1994–2004	2007
Lesley Vainikolo	NZ	-	2008

* also capped for the British and Irish Lions rugby union team.

— ERIKA BARES ALL —

Michael O'Brien was the first recorded streaker at a rugby international when he disrobed during a match between England and Wales at Twickenham on 16 March 1974. More memorably, Erika Roe and Sarah Bennett performed a joint streak at half-time during England's match with Australia at Twickenham on 2 January 1982. Despite England's hard-fought 15–11 victory, 24-year-old Erika stole the headlines the following day – thanks no doubt to her eye-catching 40-inch chest!

— THE CALCUTTA PLATE —

On 5 March 1988 England beat Scotland 9–6 at Murrayfield to win the Calcutta Cup. Later that evening the famous old trophy went missing from the Edinburgh hotel where England were staying. When, a few hours later, the cup reappeared it was found to be badly damaged. An enquiry was launched into the episode, which decided that the two main culprits were England number 8 Dean Richards, a policeman by profession, and Scottish back-rower John Jeffrey. The pair were censured for their role in the affair and Richards was banned for one match by the RFU. On seeing the extent of the damage to the trophy one SRU official is said to have remarked, "It looks like we'll be playing for the Calcutta Plate from now on!"

— 30 POINTS IN A GAME —

Players who have scored 30 points in a single England match:

For England:		Result
44	Charlie Hodgson (v Romania, Twickenham, 17 Nov 2001)*	Won 134–0
36	Paul Grayson (v Tonga, Twickenham, 15 Oct 1999)	Won 101–10
35	Jonny Wilkinson (v Italy, Twickenham, 17 Feb 2001)	Won 80–23
32	Jonny Wilkinson (v Italy, Twickenham, 2 Oct 1999)	Won 67–7
30	Rob Andrew (v Canada, Twickenham, 10 Dec 1994)	Won 60–19
30	Paul Grayson (v Netherlands, Huddersfield, 14 Nov 1998)	Won 110–0
30	Jonny Wilkinson (v Wales, Twickenham, 23 Mar 2002)	Won 50–10

* Hodgson's record points haul (two tries, 14 conversions and two penalty goals) was all the more impressive as it was achieved on his England debut.

Against:		Result
34	Jannie de Beer (for South Africa, Paris, 24 Oct 1999)	Lost 21–44

Argentina's Federico Todeschini equalled the world test record for points scored in a match by a replacement when he tallied 22 points during his country's famous victory over England at Twickenham on 11 November 2006.

— MR VERSATILITY —

Three England players have won caps starting a match in four separate positions among the backs:

Mike Catt has gained 15 caps at full-back, one on the wing, 31 at centre and a further 15 caps as fly-half.

Austin Healey was capped once at full-back, 31 times on the wing, once at fly-half and 4 times at scrum-half. He is the only player since the early 1900s to start a test at both fly-half and scrum-half.

Josh Lewsey has to date won 28 caps at full-back, 26 on the wing, one at centre and two at fly-half.

— 57 OLD FARTS —

On 7 May 1995 Will Carling, the then England captain, was sacked by RFU President Dennis Easby after describing the RFU committee as "57 old farts" on the Channel Four TV programme *Fair Game*. Two days later, following sustained pressure from Carling's team-mates and statements from Rob Andrew and Dean Richards that they would decline the England captaincy if offered it, Easby relented and reinstated Carling as skipper.

— A SHORT CAP —

Joe Worsley's substitution after 9 mins in Cardiff in 2007 may seem like a short time for a cap but there are seven players who spent even less time on the pitch to earn a cap. England players permanently replaced within the first ten minutes of an international match:

Time	Player	Opponents (Venue)	Date	Replacement
2 mins	Marcus Rose	v Australia (Sydney)	23 May 1987	Jonathan Webb#
2 mins	Gareth Chilcott	v Romania (Bucharest)	13 May 1989	Jeff Probyn
3 mins	Mike Teague	v Wales (Cardiff)	18 Mar 1989	Gary Rees
*4 mins	Nick Jeavons	v Scotland (Twickenham)	21 Feb 1981	Bob Hesford
5 mins	Peter Winterbottom	v Scotland (Murrayfield)	5 Mar 1988	Gary Rees
7 mins	Dan Luger	v Wales (Cardiff)	3 Feb 2001	Austin Healey
9 mins	Tony Underwood	v South Africa (Twickenham)	5 Dec 1998	David Rees
9 mins	Joe Worsley	v Wales (Cardiff)	17 Mar 2007	Magnus Lund

* Jeavons was making his debut and was forced to retire early, and be replaced by Bob Hesford, after poking himself in the eye!
# Jonathan Webb was making his debut.

— ENGLAND LEGENDS: BILL BEAUMONT —

Bill Beaumont was at the forefront of England's revival in the late 1970s, culminating when he skippered the side to their first Grand Slam for 23 years in 1980.

Beaumont made his England debut in January 1975, coming into the team as an eleventh-hour replacement following a back injury to Roger Uttley. He lost his place after Uttley's return to fitness, but regained it on that summer's tour to Australia and was subsequently selected for 33 consecutive internationals. Cruelly, in 1982 at the age of 29, he was forced to retire due to an injury sustained while playing in the County Championship final for his beloved Lancashire.

Bill was awarded the OBE in 1982. In the same year he was banned from coaching following the RFU's ruling that payments he received for his autobiography, *Thanks to Rugby*, breached the sport's strict amateur code. Beaumont later turned his hand to broadcasting, becoming a popular team captain on the BBC's celebrity sports quiz *A Question of Sport*. He later joined the RFU management board.

"Looks like we've picked up the Bill!"

William Blackledge Beaumont OBE Factfile
Born: 9 Mar 1952 in Preston, Lancashire
Club: Fylde
Caps: 34 (W14, D3, L17)
Scoring: None
England debut: 18 Jan 1975 vs Ireland (Dublin)

— SMITH PASSES TO SMITH —

The most popular surnames of England rugby internationals:

Smith	12
Taylor	9
Scott	8
Wilson	8
Roberts	7
Williams	7
Wright	7
Bell	6
Robinson	6
Wilkinson	6
Wood	6

— AN ELDERLY CATT —

Only one England captain has been older than Mike Catt was against France at Twickenham on 11 March 2007 when skippering England for the first time. Catt was making his 68th test appearance but his first as captain and was aged 35 years 175 days. England's only older player when making his debut as skipper was Dorian West at Marseilles on 30 August 2003 for the World Cup warm-up match. West, who was leading England for his one and only occasion on his 18th test appearance was aged 35 years and 329 days.

— STANLEY, I PRESUME —

Stanley Wakefield Harris is one of the more colourful characters to have pulled on an England jersey. Born in Somerset East in South Africa, but educated at Bedford School, Stanley played for Transvaal in 1914 before enlisting in the army during World War I. He saw action as a gunnery officer in the Battle of the Somme where he was badly wounded. While he was recuperating he took up dancing and reached the final of the world ballroom dancing championships. In 1920 he turned down a place in the British team for the modern pentathlon at the Olympic Games in Antwerp, preferring instead to play rugby. A nippy winger, he was rewarded with his two England caps that same year and in 1924 toured his native South Africa with the Lions, appearing in two tests.

An all-round sportsman, Harris won the South African amateur light-heavyweight boxing title in 1921 and played polo for England.

He was alo a useful tennis player, representing South Africa in the Davis Cup and winning the All-England mixed doubles title.

During World War II he spent three and a half years as a Japanese prisoner of war, working on the notorious 'Railway of Death' in Siam (later Thailand). He was awarded the CBE in 1946, and died aged 78 in Cape Town in 1973.

— NOT BORN IN ENGLAND —

Altogether 140 players who have gained caps for England were not born in the country. On six separate occasions England have lined up with no fewer than six non-English born players in the team.

Five of these games were in 1921 and 1922. For the visits of Wales and Ireland to Twickenham in early 1921 the England team featured Edward Myers (born New York, USA), Alastair Smallwood (born Alloa, Scotland), Bruno Brown (born Brisbane, Australia), Reg Edwards (born Newport, Wales), Frank Mellish (born Rondebosch, South Africa) and Ernest Gardner (born Cardiff, Wales).

More recently, on 31 May 1997, England visited Buenos Aires to take on Argentina with a XV containing Nick Greenstock (born Dubai), Adedayo Adebayo (born Ibadan, Nigeria), Mike Catt (born Port Elizabeth, South Africa), Kyran Bracken (born Dublin, Ireland), Kevin Yates (born Medicine Hat, Canada) and Nigel Redman (born Cardiff, Wales).

— ENGLAND'S FIRST BORN —

Arthur Sumner Gibson was the first England player ever born. Gibson came into this world on 14 July 1844 in the New Forest in Hampshire, and made just one international appearance as a forward in the inaugural test match between Scotland and England in 1871. The Manchester player, who was educated at Marlborough College and Oxford University, went on to become a civil engineer and died in Berkshire in 1927.

— FIRST TO DIE —

The first English international player to die was Charles Arthur Crompton, who was killed on active service with the Royal Engineers in Bengal, India on 6 July 1875 aged 26. A forward with Blackheath, Crompton won his only cap in the very first international match between Scotland and England at Raeburn Place in 1871. He also played football for England in an unofficial international.

— NO PLACE LIKE HOME —

A complete list of all England's home grounds, and when they first hosted international action:

Ground Name	Date	Opponent	Total Tests	W	D	L
Kennington Oval	5 Feb 1872	Scotland	7	6	1	-
Whalley Range, Manchester	28 Feb 1880	Scotland	7	5	1	1
Richardson's Field, Blackheath	19 Feb 1881	Wales	1	1	-	-
Cardigan Fields, Leeds	5 Jan 1884	Wales	1	1	-	-
Rectory Field, Blackheath	1 Mar 1884	Scotland	14	8	-	6
Crown Flatt, Dewsbury	15 Feb 1890	Wales	1	-	-	1
Richmond Athletic Ground	7 Mar 1891	Scotland	10	3	-	7
Headingley, Leeds	4 Mar 1893	Scotland	1	-	-	1
Birkenhead Park	6 Jan 1894	Wales	1	1	-	-
Meanwood Road, Leeds	1 Feb 1896	Ireland	1	-	-	1
Fallowfield, Manchester	13 Mar 1897	Scotland	1	1	-	-
Kingsholm, Gloucester	6 Jan 1900	Wales	1	-	-	1
Welford Road, Leicester	8 Feb 1902	Ireland	5	3	1	1
Crystal Palace	2 Dec 1905	New Zealand	2	-	1	1
Ashton Gate, Bristol	18 Jan 1908	Wales	1	-	-	1
Twickenham	15 Jan 1910	Wales	235	157	23	65
Wembley Stadium	17 Oct 1992	Canada	1*	1	-	-
Old Trafford, Manchester	22 Nov 1997	New Zealand	1	-	-	1
McAlpine Stadium, Huddersfield	14 Nov 1998	Netherlands	2	2	-	-

* Wembley was also used for an 'away' game against Wales which England lost 31–32

— AWAY DAYS —

The away venues most visited by England:

Ground	First visited	Total P	W	D	L
Lansdowne Road, Dublin	11 Mar 1878	57	28	4	25
Murrayfield	21 Mar 1925	41	17	3	21
Cardiff Arms Park#	7 Jan 1893	40	13	2	25
Stade Colombes, Paris	1 Jan 1908	21	9	1	11
Parc des Princes, Paris	22 Mar 1906	17	10	1	6
St Helens, Swansea	16 Dec 1882	13	5	1	7
Raeburn Place, Edinburgh	27 Mar 1871	10	3	4	3
Inverleith, Edinburgh	10 Mar 1900	10	6	1	3
Stade de France, Paris	7 Feb 1998	10	3	-	7
Concord Oval, Sydney	23 May 1987	4	2	-	2
Stadio Flaminio, Rome	18 Mar 2000	5	5	-	-
Newlands, Cape Town	11 Jun 1994	4	1	-	3
Ferrocarril Oeste, Buenos Aires	30 May 1981	4	2	1	1
Suncorp Stadium, Brisbane	6 Jun 1998	4	2	-	2
Eden Park, Auckland	25 May 1963	4	1	-	3
Loftus Versfeld, Pretoria	4 Jun 1994	4	1	-	3
Telstra Stadium, Sydney*	26 Jun 1999	4	2	-	2

* Known as Stadium Australia for the 1999 match.
#including Millennium Stadium from 1999 to date

England have played test matches at five different grounds in Sydney, Australia – a record for one opposing city; losing 9–18 at the Sydney Sports Ground in 1963, losing 9-16 at the Sydney Cricket Ground in 1975, winning two and losing two at Concord Oval (1987–88), losing twice at the Sydney Football (now Aussie) Stadium (15–40 in 1991 and 6–25 in 1997), and winning two and losing two at Stadium Australia (now known as Telstra Stadium).

— QUICK OUT OF THE BLOCKS —

England's fastest recorded tries from the start of a match:

10 seconds	Leo Price	v Wales (Twickenham)	20 Jan 1923
23 seconds	Jonathan Webb	v Ireland (Twickenham)	1 Feb 1992
61 seconds	Will Carling	v Wales (Twickenham)	7 Mar 1992
75 seconds	Fred Chapman	v Wales (Twickenham)	15 Jan 1910
78 seconds	Josh Lewsey	v France (Paris)	13 Oct 2007

Rob Andrew scored England's quickest ever drop goal after 47 seconds on his debut against Romania in January 1985.

— POSTPONED —

Just nine England games have been postponed. The first was way back on 3 February 1879 when Ireland were the visitors to the Oval Cricket Ground. However, hard frost prevented any play and the match was eventually rescheduled for 24 March when England ran out winners by a score of 2 goals, 1 drop goal and 2 tries to nil.

Only two of England's Twickenham tests have needed rescheduling. Ireland were due to visit on 9 February 1952 but all sport was halted due to the untimely death of King George VI. The match was rescheduled for 29 March with England winning 3–0. On 17 January 1987 heavy snow forced the cancellation of Scotland's visit to Twickenham for the opening match in that season's Five Nations championship. The match was finally played on 4 April, England winning 21–12.

Most recently, an outbreak of foot and mouth disease in mainland Britain led to the postponement of England's match with Ireland in Dublin on 24 March 2001. When the match was eventually played on 20 October England blew their chances of winning the Grand Slam by going down 14–20 to the home side.

— WARTIME INTERNATIONALS —

During World War II England played 24 international games, none of which have ever been included as capped matches. Here's the full list of these encounters:

— RED CROSS INTERNATIONALS —

1939–40

9 Mar	Wales	Cardiff	Won 18–9
30 Mar	Wales	Gloucester	Won 17–3

— SERVICES INTERNATIONALS —

1941–42

7 Mar	Wales	Swansea	Lost 12–17
21 Mar	Scotland	Inverleith	Lost 6–21
28 Mar	Wales	Gloucester	Lost 3–9
14 Apr	Scotland	Wembley	Lost 5–8

1942–43

7 Nov	Wales	Swansea	Lost 7–11
27 Feb	Scotland	Inverleith	Won 29–6
20 Mar	Wales	Gloucester	Lost 7–34
10 Apr	Scotland	Leicester	Won 24–19

1943–44

20 Nov	Wales	Swansea	Lost 9–11
26 Feb	Scotland	Murrayfield	Won 23–13
18 Mar	Scotland	Leicester	Won 27–15
8 Apr	Wales	Gloucester	Won 20–8

1944–45

25 Nov	Wales	Swansea	Lost 11–28
24 Feb	Scotland	Leicester	Lost 11–18
17 Mar	Scotland	Murrayfield	Won 16–5
7 Apr	Wales	Gloucester	Lost 9–24

— VICTORY INTERNATIONALS —

1945–46

24 Nov	Kiwis	Twickenham	Lost 3–18
19 Jan	Wales	Cardiff	Won 25–13
6 Feb	Ireland	Twickenham	Won 14–6
23 Feb	Wales	Twickenham	Lost 0–3
16 Mar	Scotland	Twickenham	Won 12–8
13 Apr	Scotland	Murrayfield	Lost 0–27

— LET THERE BE LIGHT —

England's first games under floodlights were played during the 1995 World Cup in Durban, South Africa, when Argentina, Italy and Samoa were the opponents on 27 and 31 May and 4 June respectively.

Floodlights were first used at Twickenham for an international against South Africa on 18 November 1995.

The latest ever kick-off for a Twickenham test is 6pm: against the United States and Canada in World Cup warm-up matches in August 1999 and against Scotland in the Six Nations Championship on 19 March 2005.

Clearly, the Rugby Football Union has come a long way since it prohibited floodlit rugby in 1933, maintaining that it was "not in the best interests of the game".

— ENGLAND AT THE FIRST RUGBY WORLD CUP: 1987 —

Games and Scorers:
Pool 1

23 May	Australia	Sydney	L 6–19	t: Harrison. c: Webb
30 May	Japan	Sydney	W 60–7	t: Harrison 3, Underwood 2, Rees, Salmon, Richards, Simms, Redman. c: Webb 7 p: Webb 2
3 June	USA	Sydney	W 34–6	t: Winterbottom 2, Harrison, Dooley. c: Webb 3. p: Webb 4

RWC Pool 1 Table:

Nation	P	W	D	L	F	A	Pts	Tries
Australia	3	3	0	0	108	41	6	18
England	3	2	0	1	100	32	4	15
United States	3	1	0	2	39	99	2	5
Japan	3	0	0	3	48	123	0	7

Quarter-final

8 June	Wales	Brisbane	L 3–16	p: Webb

Squad and Appearances:
Manager: Mike Weston. Coach: Martin Green.
Captain: Mike Harrison.
Rob Andrew (Wasps) J(r)/US; Mark Bailey (Wasps) US; Steve Bainbridge (Fylde) J/US; Gareth Chilcott (Bath) J/US/W(r); Fran Clough (Orrell)

J(r)/US; Huw Davies (Wasps)*; Graham Dawe (Bath) US; Wade Dooley (Fylde) Au/US/W; David Egerton (Bath); Jon Hall (Bath); Richard Harding (Bristol) Au/J/W; Mike Harrison (Wakefield) Au/J/US/W; Richard Hill (Bath) US; Brian Moore (Nottingham) Au/J/W; Gary Pearce (Northampton Saints) Au/US/W; Jeff Probyn (Wasps); Nigel Redman (Bath) Au/J/W; Gary Rees (Nottingham) Au/J/US/W; Paul Rendall (Wasps) Au/J/W; Dean Richards (Leicester Tigers) Au/J/US/W; Marcus Rose (Harlequins) Au; Jamie Salmon (Harlequins) Au/J/US/W; Kevin Simms (Wasps) Au/J/W; Mickey Skinner (Harlequins)*; Rory Underwood (Leicester Tigers) Au/J/W; Jon Webb (Bristol) Au(r)/J/US/W; Peter Williams (Orrell) Au/J/W; Peter Winterbottom (Headingley) Au/J/US/W. Appearances as a replacement marked with (r).

* Due to injuries, Davies and Skinner were late inclusions.

Scoring:

Name	T	C	P	D	Pts
Jon Webb	-	11	7	-	43
Mike Harrison	5	-	-	-	20
Rory Underwood	2	-	-	-	8
Peter Winterbottom	2	-	-	-	8
Wade Dooley	1	-	-	-	4
Nigel Redman	1	-	-	-	4
Gary Rees	1	-	-	-	4
Dean Richards	1	-	-	-	4
Jamie Salmon	1	-	-	-	4
Kevin Simms	1	-	-	-	4
TOTALS	15	11	7	0	103
AGAINST	7	4	4	0	48

— MAN IN THE MIDDLE CROCKED —

There have been four recorded instances of a referee at an England match having to be replaced due to injury:

Date	Opponent (Venue)	Referee	Replaced by	Min
28 Feb 1970	Wales (Twickenham)	Robert Calmet	Johnny Johnson	HT
20 Mar 1999	France (Twickenham)	Colin Hawke	Jim Fleming	HT
7 Apr 2001	France (Twickenham)	Tappe Henning	David McHugh	48
24 Nov 2001	South Africa (Twickenham)	Stuart Dickinson	David McHugh	12

— SECOND HALF HEROES —

The biggest half-time deficit England have reversed to win a match is just nine points against Argentina in Buenos Aires on 22 June 2002. Following a penalty kicking dual between Gonzalo Quesada and Charlie Hodgson which was won 4–1 by the Puma, England were trailing 3–12 at the break. However, second half tries by Ben Kay and Phil Christophers helped England win the match 26–18.

England produced an even better second-half performance against Ireland at Twickenham in 1988. 3–0 down at the break and without injured skipper and scrum-half Nigel Melville, who was carried off on the stroke of half-time when he fell awkwardly in a tackle, the home side responded with 35 unanswered second-half points. Stars of the show were replacement scrum-half Richard Harding and Chris Oti, who helped himself to a hat-trick of tries. Melville, meanwhile, was never capped again, while the England fans celebrated the dramatic turnaround with a first rendition of 'Swing Low, Sweet Chariot.'

— THE TEN TRY CLUB —

The full list of players who have scored ten or more tries for England:

Player		Career	Tries	Caps	Tries per game				
					1	2	3	4	5
1	Rory Underwood	1984–1996	49	85	21	10	1	-	1
2=	Will Greenwood	1997–2005	31	50+5	14	7	1	-	-
2=	Ben Cohen	2000–2006	31	54+3	16	6	1	-	-
4	Jerry Guscott	1989–1999	30	62+3	13	3	1	2	-
5	Jason Robinson	2001–2007	28	47+4	10	4	2	1	-
6	Dan Luger	1998–2003	24	32+6	15	3	1	-	-
7	Josh Lewsey	1998–2007	22	53+2	9	4	-	-	1
8	Cyril Lowe	1913–1923	18	25	8	2	2	-	-
9	Lawrence Dallaglio	1995–2007	17	70+15	15	1	-	-	-
10=	Neil Back	1994–2005	16	66	10	1	-	1	-
10=	Matt Dawson	1995–2006	16	55+22	12	2	-	-	-
12	Austin Healey	1997–2003	15	37+14	6	3	1	-	-
13=	Mark Cueto	2004–2007	13	24	8	1	1	-	-
13=	Tony Underwood	1992–1998	13	27	7	3	-	-	-
13=	Iain Balshaw	2000–2008	13	26+9	7	3	-	-	-
13=	Mike Tindall	2000–2008	13	52+4	11	1	-	-	-
17=	Will Carling	1988–1997	12	72	10	1	-	-	-
17=	Richard Hill	1997–2005	12	68+3	12	-	-	-	-
19=	John Birkett	1906–1912	10	21	6	2	-	-	-
19=	David Duckham	1969–1976	10	36	6	2	-	-	-
19=	Matt Perry	1997–2001	10	34+2	6	2	-	-	-

— PLAYERS UNDER SIR CLIVE —

In his 83–match tenure as England supremo, Sir Clive Woodward named 108 different players in his matchday squads of whom all but eight had some game time.

Jason Leonard was selected most often: 47 times as a starter and 19 further times on the replacements bench. Neil Back was next with 64 appearances, followed by Richard Hill with 63, including a record sixty occasions in the starting XV.

— MOST TRIES WITHOUT REPLY —

England scored an impressive total of 31 tries from November 2001 until February 2002 without any of their opponents crossing the 'whitewash'. Between Phil Waugh scoring for the Wallabies at Twickenham on 10 November 2001 and Ronan O'Gara touching down for Ireland at Twickenham on 16 February 2002, England defeated Romania 134–0, South Africa 29–9 and Scotland 29–3.

Less happily, England conceded 14 tries without scoring any themselves in 1998. The dismal run included 11 tries in one match by Australia in Brisbane on 6 June 1998.

Tries for

No	From	To
31	10 Nov 2001 Phil Waugh (Australia)	16 Feb 2002 Ronan O'Gara (Ireland)
21	28 Feb 1880 Hopper Brown (Scotland)	19 Mar 1881 Robert Ainslie (Scotland)
19	4 July 1998 Stefan Terblanche (S Africa)	5 Dec 1998 Pieter Rossouw (S Africa)
18	23 Feb 1874 John Finlay (Scotland)	30 Jan 1880 John Cuppaidge (Ireland)

Tries against

No	From	To
14	4 Apr 1998 Phil de Glanville (v Ireland)	20 Jun 1998 Richard Cockerill (NZ)
13	19 Feb 1904 Elliott Vivyan (v Scotland)	11 Feb 1905 Syd Coopper (Ireland)
13	17 Mar 1984 Dusty Hare (v France)	5 Jan 1995 Simon Smith (v Romania)

— BETTER SOLDIER THAN CAPTAIN —

Leicester hooker Dorian West skippered England just once, a narrow 16–17 defeat to France in Marseille in a World Cup warm-up match in August 2003. Perhaps West should never have been promoted from the ranks – in his other nine international starts, England won the lot!

— COTTON'S GREATEST EVER TEAM —

In 1996, Fran Cotton, the stalwart England prop and manager of the 1997 British Lions, was asked to name his all-time greatest ever England team as part of the RFU's 125th anniversary celebrations. His team lined up as follows:

15	David Caplan	Headingley
14	Rory Underwood	Leicester
13	Jeff Butterfield	Northampton
12	Jerry Guscott	Bath
11	Mike Slemen	Liverpool
10	Alan Old	Middlesbrough
9	Dickie Jeeps	Northampton
1	Fran Cotton	Sale
2	Peter Wheeler	Leicester
3	Ron Jacobs	Northampton
4	Paul Ackford	Harlequins
5	Bill Beaumont (capt)	Fylde
6	Tony Neary	Broughton Park
8	Peter Dixon	Gosforth
7	Peter Robbins	Coventry

— ENGLAND LEGENDS: WILL CARLING —

Will Carling was brought into the England set up at the age of 22 by manager Geoff Cooke, and within ten months the then army captain was handed the skipper's armband. In Carling's seven years in charge England had an unprecedented period of success against northern hemisphere opposition, winning four Five Nations titles. Even more impressively, Carling became the only skipper to lead his country to three Grand Slams. The first name on the teamsheet for many years, his record run for England of 44 successive matches was halted when an ankle injury prevented his appearance against Italy during the 1995 Rugby World Cup in Durban.

Carling retired from international rugby in 1997, finishing his career as England's most capped centre.

Despite his many successes, there was a perception that his own game often suffered because of the burdens of captaincy. However, his record of 44 wins in 59 matches as captain is without equal in England history. Following retirement, Carling developed a business career as a corporate motivator and he has also worked as a TV pundit. He was awarded an OBE in 1992.

Three-time Grand Slam skipper, Will Carling

William David Charles Carling OBE Factfile
Born: 12 Dec 1965 in Bradford-on-Avon, Wiltshire
Clubs: Harlequins
Caps: 72 (W53, D1, L18)
Scoring: 12 tries – 54 pts
England debut: 16 Jan 1988 vs France (Paris)

— ENGLAND AT THE SECOND RUGBY WORLD CUP: 1991 —

Games and Scorers:
Pool 1

3 Oct	N Zealand	Twickenham	L 12–18	p: Webb 3. d: Andrew
8 Oct	Italy	Twickenham	W 36–6	t: Guscott 2, Underwood, Webb. c: Webb 4. p: Webb 4
11 Oct	USA	Twickenham	W 37–9	t: Underwood 2, Carling, Skinner, Heslop. c: Webb 4. p: Webb 3

RWC Pool 1 Table:

Nation	P	W	D	L	F	A	Pts	Tries
New Zealand	3	3	0	0	95	39	9	13
England	3	2	0	1	85	33	7	9
Italy	3	1	0	2	57	76	5	7
United States	3	0	0	3	24	113	3	2

Quarter-final

19 Oct	France	Paris	W 19–10	t: Underwood, Carling. c: Webb. p: Webb 3

Semi-final

26 Oct	Scotland	Murrayfield	W 9–6	p: Webb 2. d: Andrew

Final

2 Nov	Australia	Twickenham	L 6–12	p: Webb 2

Squad and Appearances:
Manager: Geoff Cooke. Coach: Roger Uttley.
Captain: Will Carling.
Paul Ackford (Harlequins) NZ/It/F/S/Au; Rob Andrew (Wasps) NZ/It/US/F/S/Au; Will Carling (Harlequins) NZ/It/US/F/S/Au; Wade Dooley (Preston Grasshoppers) NZ/US/F/S/Au; Jerry Guscott (Bath) NZ/It/F/S/Au; Simon Halliday (Harlequins) US/S/Au; Nigel Heslop

(Orrell) US/F; Richard Hill (Bath) NZ/It/US/F/S/Au; Simon Hodgkinson (Nottingham) US; Jason Leonard (Harlequins) NZ/It/US/F/S/Au; Brian Moore (Harlequins) NZ/It/F/S/Au; Dewi Morris (Orrell); John Olver (Northampton Saints) US; Chris Oti (Wasps) NZ/It; Gary Pearce (Northampton Saints) US; David Pears (Harlequins); Jeff Probyn (Askeans) NZ/It/F/S/Au; Nigel Redman (Bath) It/US; Gary Rees (Nottingham) US; Paul Rendall (Askeans) It(r); Dean Richards (Leicester Tigers) NZ/It/US; Mickey Skinner (Harlequins) US/F/S/Au; Mike Teague (Gloucester) NZ/It/F/S/Au; Rory Underwood (Leicester Tigers) NZ/It/US/F/S/Au; Jon Webb (Bath) NZ/It/F/S/Au; Peter Winterbottom (Harlequins) NZ/It/F/S/Au. Appearances as a replacement marked with (r).

Scoring:					
Name	T	C	P	D	Pts
Jon Webb	1	5	14	-	56
Simon Hodgkinson	-	4	3	-	17
Rory Underwood	4	-	-	-	16
Will Carling	2	-	-	-	8
Jerry Guscott	2	-	-	-	8
Rob Andrew	-	-	-	2	6
Nigel Heslop	1	-	-	-	4
Mickey Skinner	1	-	-	-	4
TOTALS	11	9	17	2	119
AGAINST	5	4	11	0	61

— FOUR SLAMS —

In 2003 Jason Leonard won a fourth Grand Slam title (his others were in 1991, 1992 and 1995), equalling fellow England players W.J.A. 'Dave' Davies, Cyril Lowe (1913, 14, 21 and 1923) and Ron Cove-Smith (1921, 23, 24 and 1928) as the only other players from any country to have achieved this feat. Of these only Cyril Lowe played in every possible match on his four successful Grand Slam campaigns.

— ENGLAND LEGENDS: PETER WHEELER —

A world-class and ultra competitive hooker, Peter Wheeler was the mainstay of the England front row for ten seasons and led the national side in 1983–84. Wheeler was from the classic mould of tight forwards who are just as effective in the loose. Fast about the field, he could handle and kick, both for touch and at goal.

Although he went on England's tour of the Far East in 1971, Wheeler did not win his first cap against France until 1975. A serious neck injury in the next game of that season, against Wales, interrupted his career, but he recovered to become a permanent fixture at hooker. Along with Graham Price and Fran Cotton he was part of a British Lions front row in New Zealand in 1977 which demolished the All Blacks, but lost the test series 3–1.

Wheeler played in England's 1980 Grand Slam team, and was later made captain of his country. In 1983, just a week before his 36th birthday, he led the side to their first victory over New Zealand at Twickenham since 1936.

Currently chief executive at Leicester Tigers and one of the sport's great administrators, Wheeler has managed to pull off a difficult balancing act, gaining the respect of both modern-day players and officialdom.

Peter John Wheeler Factfile
Born: 26 Nov 1948 in South Norwood, London
Clubs: Old Brockleians, Leicester
Caps: 41 (W17, D2, L22)
Scoring: None
England debut: 1 Feb 1975 vs France (Twickenham)

— SEE-SAW THRILLERS —

Two of the most exciting England matches ever were against Scotland in 1994 and Ireland in 2005. On both occasions the lead changed an incredible six times – a record for an England match.

At Murrayfield on 5 February 1994, England scored the opening points with a Jon Callard penalty strike after five minutes before Scotland countered with a Rob Wainwright try on the half hour to take the lead. Three minutes after the break Gavin Hastings, the Scottish skipper, kicked the home side further ahead with a penalty. Two penalties by Callard then helped England regain lead on the hour, by the slim margin of 9–8. The penalty kicking duel continued with Hastings and Callard exchanging successful kicks, before Gregor Townsend dropped an 80th minute goal to take Scotland ahead at

14–12. Callard wasn't finished, however, and the Bath full-back slotted the winning penalty goal in injury time.

The match between Ireland and England at Lansdowne Road on 27 February 2005 was equally thrilling. Ronan O'Gara kicked an early drop goal before Martin Corry powered over for a try converted by Charlie Hodgson to give the visitors a 7–3 lead. However, two O'Gara penalties on nine and 12 minutes edged the Irishmen back in front. Hodgson then regained the lead for England with a 24th minute penalty goal. Either side of half-time O'Gara and Hodgson swapped drop goals, as the lead twice changed hands again. Finally, in the 58th minute, Brian O'Driscoll swooped for the decisive try and the sixth lead change of the afternoon. O'Gara's conversion confirmed a 19–13 victory for the men in green.

— JUNIOR NATIONS —

England didn't award full caps for matches against junior nations until the inaugural World Cup in Australia and New Zealand in 1987. Games where the minnows awarded full caps but England didn't are as follows:

Date	Opponents	Venue	Result
30 Sep 1967	Canada	Vancouver	Won 29–0
24 Sep 1971	Japan	Osaka	Won 27–19
28 Sep 1971	Japan	Tokyo	Won 6–3
28 Aug 1973	Fiji	Suva	Won 13–12
15 Oct 1977	United States	Twickenham	Won 37–11
14 Oct 1978	Argentina	Twickenham	Drew 13–13
13 May 1979	Japan	Osaka	Won 21–19
20 May 1979	Japan	Tokyo	Won 38–18
29 May 1979	Fiji	Suva	Won 19–7
1 Jun 1979	Tonga	Nuku'alofa	Won 37–17
29 May 1982	Canada	Burnaby	Won 43–6
19 Jun 1982	United States	Hartford	Won 59–0
16 Oct 1982	Fiji	Twickenham	Won 60–19
15 Oct 1983	Canada	Twickenham	Won 27–0
10 May 1986	Italy	Rome	Drew 15–15
11 Oct 1986	Japan	Twickenham	Won 39–12
7 Sep 1991	Soviet Union	Twickenham	Won 53–0
29 May 1993	Canada	Burnaby	Lost 12–15
5 Jun 1993	Canada	Nepean	Won 19–14
19 Jun 2005	Canada	Edmonton	Won 29–5 (Churchill Cup semi-final)

NB: The game between an England XV and Italy XV at Rovigo in 1990 is NOT included as Italy did not award caps on the day either.

— ENGLAND'S 1000th CAPPED PLAYER —

In a special non-Championship game in March 1971 to celebrate the first ever test match between England and Scotland 100 years earlier, Richmond lock Chris Ralston became the 999th England player to be capped.

England's next test match, on 17 April 1971, was another one-off game to commemorate the Centenary of the RFU and saw England take on an RFU President's XV containing 15 of the best players from overseas – 5 New Zealanders, 4 Australians, 4 South Africans and 2 Frenchmen. England gave debuts to two players in the back-row: so Coventry's Roger Creed and Harlequin Peter Dixon have the honour of jointly becoming England's 1000th and 1001st players. It was to be Creed's only cap but Dixon went on to gain 21 more over the next seven years.

— WHITE LINE FEVER —

England scored at least one try in 46 successive tests between 1911 and 1927. The impressive run began on 18 March 1911 with a 13–8 win over Scotland at Twickenham and continued until a 0–3 defeat to France at the Stade Colombes in Paris on 2 April 1927. Of the 46 games played, England won 34, drew three and lost nine.

England have twice conceded tries in 19 successive matches. The first such run started with a 13–17 loss to Wales on 28 February 1970 and only ended when England prevented the Wallabies from getting a try in a 20–3 win at Twickenham on 17 November 1973. The second began with victory over Scotland on 16 March 1985 and ended when Scotland were restricted to two penalty goals in a 9–6 win at Murrayfield on 5 March 1988.

— FIVE/SIX NATIONS TROPHY —

For many years the winners of the International Championship didn't receive a trophy to mark their achievement. However, in 1993 the Earl of Westmorland commissioned a sterling silver trophy which was first presented to the winners later that year. Designed by James Brent-Ward and made by a team of eight silversmiths from the London firm William Comyns, the trophy is worth around £55,000. Originally silver on the inside, the winners' habit of pouring champagne into the trophy has so corroded the lining that it is now gold plated.

The Six Nations trophy has 15 side panels representing the

individual members of the winning team and three handles representing the three officials. The cup's capacity is 375 centilitres – sufficient for five bottles of champagne! Within the mahogany base there is a concealed drawer containing six alternate finials, which can be screwed onto the detachable lid. Each finial is a silver replica of one of the six national team emblems.

England have won the trophy on five occasions: in 1995, 1996, 2000, 2001 and 2003.

— WHITE LINE DROUGHT —

The longest tryless spell England have endured stretched for five complete games, starting on 15 March 1958 with a 3–3 draw against Scotland at Murrayfield and ending in a 14–6 win over Wales at Twickenham on 16 January 1960. England's next worst barren run consisted of four complete games, beginning with the 3–4 loss to France at Twickenham on 19 February 1977 and ending in a 15–0 win against Scotland at Murrayfield on 4 March 1978.

The most consecutive games England have denied their opponents a try is ten. This fortress-like run began with victory over Ireland at the Oval on 15 February 1875 and only ended when the same opponents crossed the line at Lansdowne Road nearly five years later on 30 January 1880.

— KEEP THE HOME FIRES BURNING —

In the winter of 1892/93 Britain was gripped by a severe freeze which led to the cancellation of numerous sporting fixtures. With the Arms Park pitch frozen solid, despite being covered by a protective layer of straw, there seemed little chance that England's march with Wales on 7 January 1893 could go ahead. However, on the night before the match, Cardiff committeeman Bill Shepherd enlisted a group of men to light 500 braziers, under which stood some 40 boiler plates to spread the heat. By 11am on Saturday morning the makeshift heaters had consumed 18 tons of coal and left blackened patches on the turf, but the endeavours of the volunteers allowed the match to go ahead. The Welshmen's efforts proved especially worthwhile, as they saw their side win a thrilling match 12–11.

Some spectators, though, were under the impression that the match had finished in a draw. At the time, the Welsh Rugby Union was conducting an experiment in club rugby in which three points were awarded for a try, compared to two points in the other home countries. Had the Welsh system been applied in this particular international then the result would have been a 14-all draw. The International Board eventually upgraded the value of a try to three points the following year.

— DASHWOOD, BADGER AND NERO —

England internationals with unusual middle names:

Adedayo **Adeyemi** Adebayo
Alfred **Rimbault** Aslett
Harold **Dingwall** Bateson
William **Blackledge** Beaumont
Barzillai **Beckerleg** Bennetts
Godfrey **Mohun** Carey
William **Inkersole** Cheesman
Stanley George **Ulick** Considine
Lawrence **Bruno Nero** Dallaglio
Aubrey **Osler** Dowson
John **Horncastle** Eddison
William Robert **Badger** Fletcher
Frank **Dashwood** Fowler
Geoffrey Robert **d'Aubrey** Hosking
William Henry **Heap** Hutchison
Michael **Rose** Lipman
Daniel **Darko** Luger
Osbert **Gadesden** Mackie
William **Octavius** Moberly
Elliot **Tenint** Nicholson
Stephen **Oziegbe** Ojomoh
Henry **Rangi** Paul
Walter **Lacy Yea** Rogers
Frank **Sholl** Scott
Christopher **Champain** Tanner
Alexander **Findlater** Todd
Peveril **Barton Reiby** William-Powlett
Walter **Carandini** Wilson
Samuel **Moses** James Woods
Cyril **Carne Glenton** Wright

— BORN IN TWICKENHAM —

Bob Mordell, the Rosslyn Park flanker, was born in Twickenham on 2 July 1951. He gained his only cap for England across "town" on the flank against Wales on 4 February 1978. He had previously played for Wasps and appeared in the 1976 cup final for Rosslyn Park before signing rugby league forms for Kent Invicta and later Oldham RL.

The only other test player born in Twickenham was Peter Stagg, a giant Sale lock, who stood 6 foot 10 in (2.05m) and gained 28 caps for Scotland between 1965–70, including two games at HQ in 1965 and 1967.

Martin Regan, the fly-half who won 12 caps for England between 1953–56 went to school at St Mary's College Twickenham, as did John Palmer, the Maltese born Bath centre who gained 3 caps between 1984–86.

— TRAITORS XV —

A team of England-born players capped for another country:

Position	Name (adopted country, caps)	Birthplace
Full-back:	John Gallagher (New Zealand, 18)	London
Wing:	Simon Geoghegan (Ireland, 37)	Knebworth
Centre:	Rob Henderson (Ireland, 29)	Dover
Centre:	Tom Shanklin (Wales, 33)	Harrow
Wing:	Phil Crowe (Australia, 6)	Westminster
Fly-half:	Ian McGeechan (Scotland, 32)	Leeds
Scrum-half:	Rupert Moon (Wales, 24)	Birmingham
Prop:	Dave Hilton (Scotland, 42)	Bristol
Hooker:	Mike Luke (Canada, 16)	Cornwall
Prop:	David Sole (Scotland, 44)	London
Lock:	Glyn Llewellyn (Wales, 9)	Bradford-on-Avon
Lock:	Peter Stagg (Scotland, 28)	Twickenham
Flanker:	Philip Matthews (Ireland, 38)	Gloucester
Flanker:	Paul Ringer (Wales, 8)	Leeds
No 8:	Nick Mallett (South Africa, 2)	Haileybury

— SHORT SIGHTED —

Bill Redwood gained two caps for England at scrum-half in 1968 despite the fact that he was blind in one eye. The Bristolian scored a try on his debut against Wales at Twickenham, but lasted just 30 minutes in the next test against Ireland before having to leave the field with concussion. With no replacements allowed at the time, Peter Bell moved from back-row to scrum-half and England did well to draw the match 9–9.

— OVERSEAS TEST PLAYING TOURS —

England's overseas tours where at least one test match was played:

Year	To	Tour games				Tests matches				Total games			
		P	W	D	L	P	W	D	L	P	W	D	L
1963	New Zealand/Australia	3	1	-	2	3	-	-	3	6	1	-	5
1972	South Africa	6	5	1	-	1	1	-	-	7	6	1	-
1973	Fiji/New Zealand	4	1	-	3	1	1	-	-	5	2	-	3
1975	Australia	6	4	-	2	2	-	-	2	8	4	-	4
1981	Argentina	5	5	-	-	2	1	1	-	7	6	1	-
1984	South Africa	5	4	1	-	2	-	-	2	7	4	1	2
1985	New Zealand	5	4	-	1	2	-	-	2	7	4	-	3
1988	Australia/Fiji	6	5	-	1	3	1	-	2	9	6	-	3
1990	Argentina	5	2	-	3	2	1	-	1	7	3	-	4
1991	Australia/Fiji	5	2	-	3	2	1	-	1	7	3	-	4
1994	South Africa	6	2	-	4	2	1	-	1	8	3	-	5
1997	Australia	-	-	-	-	1	-	-	1	1	-	-	1
1997	Argentina	4	3	-	1	2	1	-	1	6	4	-	2
1998	Australia/New Zealand/ South Africa	3	-	-	3	4	-	-	4	7	-	-	7
1999	Australia	1	1	-	-	1	-	-	1	2	1	-	1
2000	South Africa	3	3	-	-	2	1	-	1	5	4	-	1
2001	USA/Canada	2	2	-	-	3	3	-	-	5	5	-	-
2002	Argentina	1	-	-	1	1	1	-	-	2	1	-	1
2003	New Zealand/Australia	1	1	-	-	2	2	-	-	3	3	-	-
2004	New Zealand/Australia	-	-	-	-	3	-	-	3	3	-	-	3
2006	Australia	-	-	-	-	2	-	-	2	2	-	-	2
2007	South Africa	-	-	-	-	2	-	-	2	2	-	-	2
2008	New Zealand	-	-	-	-	2	-	-	2	2	-	-	2

— HAT-TRICK AND GOODBYE —

Howard Marshall had a storming match on his England debut against Wales at Cardiff on 7 January 1893. The Blackheath fly-half bagged a hat-trick of tries, but his efforts weren't enough to prevent Wales winning the game 12–11. Surprisingly, Marshall was never picked to play for his country again and remains the only England player to have finished on the losing side after scoring three tries.

The circumstances behind Wales' winning score are the subject of folklore, especially in the Valleys. England had led throughout the match and were 11–9 ahead when they were penalised 30 yards out and close to the touch line. Welsh skipper Arthur Gould instructed full-back Billy Bancroft to place the ball and kick the goal. However, Bancroft refused saying he would prefer to use a drop kick instead. Eventually, Bancroft won the argument and dropped the ball between the uprights for the winning points – the first successful penalty goal ever kicked in a test match.

Marshall, meanwhile, is one of a select band of eighteen players to have scored a try on their only appearance for England. Of this group, the first 15 got on the scoresheet before 1989. Since then, only Mark Linnett, Steve Hanley and Hugh Vyvyan have marked their single international appearances with a try.

— PLEASE DON'T PICK ME! —

Barney Solomon had a superb England debut in Twickenham's first international match in January 1910, scoring a try in England's 11–6 win. The Redruth centre then asked the selectors not to pick him again because he felt it was simply too far to travel from his home in Cornwall to matches in London.

— A TON UP —

England have topped the century mark of points in five test matches:

Result	Opponent (Venue)	Date
Won 110–0	v Netherlands (Huddersfield)	14 Nov 1998
Won 106–8	v USA (Twickenham)	21 Aug 1999
Won 101–10	v Tonga (Twickenham)	15 Oct 1999
Won 134–0	v Romania (Twickenham)	17 Nov 2001
Won 111–13	v Uruguay (Brisbane)	2 Nov 2003

— A HALF-CENTURY AGAINST —

England have conceded 50 or more points on just five occasions:

Result	Opponent (Venue)	Date
Lost 0–76	v Australia (Brisbane)	6 Jun 1998
Lost 22–64	v New Zealand (Dunedin)	20 Jun 1998
Lost 15–51	v Australia (Brisbane)	26 Jun 2004
Lost 10–58	v South Africa (Bloemfontein)	26 May 2007
Lost 22–55	v South Africa (Pretoria)	2 Jun 2007

— ALL WHITE! —

The reason that England wear white shirts and shorts is not recorded in RFU minutes but it seems entirely reasonable that it was because those were also the colours of Rugby School. Either way, the colour stuck because it is the only colour England have worn for all but two of their 580 matches.

The exceptions were when they wore blue shirts and white shorts for the Rugby World Cup play-off game against Fiji at Twickenham on 20 October 1999, whilst the other instance was a dark blue shirt with multiple narrow white and red bands and dark blue shorts worn for the special celebration match to mark Australia's centenary in test rugby in Sydney on 26 June 1999. This game was the only occasion that England have not worn white shorts for an international.

Incidentally, the first time England wore dark blue socks was against Scotland at Murrayfield in 1931. Prior to this players wore their own club socks whilst turning out for their country.

England's basic kit of white shirts, white shorts and dark blue socks was worn without modification from 1931 until the 1991 Rugby World Cup, when England introduced other colours for the first time: their shirt at the tournament featuring narrow blue and red bands on the right sleeve, a blue collar and red neck opening. The first time a round collar was employed on the shirts was for the triumphant 2003 Rugby World Cup competition in Australia.

In 2007 the RFU unveiled a radical new kit with a bold red swoosh which was reflected on the shorts and red and white stocks replaced the traditional dark blue ones. England will also wear a non-white or blue shirt for the first time as the blue away kit has been replaced by a more 'St. George-like' red jersey.

— FOUR TRIES IN A GAME —

For England:		Position
5	Daniel Lambert (v France, Richmond, 5 Jan 1907)*	Wing
5	Rory Underwood (v Fiji, Twickenham, 4 Nov 1989)	Wing
5	Josh Lewsey (v Uruguay, Brisbane, 2 Nov 2003)	Full-back
4	George Burton (v Wales, 19 Feb 1881)	Forward
4	Arthur Hudson (v France, Paris, 22 Mar 1906)	Wing
4	Ronald Poulton (v France, Paris, 13 Apr 1914)	Centre
4	Chris Oti (v Romania, Bucharest, 13 May 1989)	Wing
4	Jeremy Guscott (v Netherlands, Huddersfield, 14 Nov 1998)	Centre

4	Neil Back (v Netherlands, Huddersfield, 14 Nov 1998)r	Flanke
4	Jeremy Guscott (v USA, Twickenham, 21 Aug 1999)	Centre
4	Jason Robinson (v Romania, Twickenham, 17 Nov 2001)	Full-back

* Test debut

Against:

4	Willie Llewellyn (for Wales, Swansea, 7 Jan 1889)	Wing
4	Duncan McGregor (for N Zealand, Crystal Palace, 2 Dec 1905)	Wing
4	Maurice Richards (for Wales, Cardiff, 12 Apr 1969)	Wing
4	Jonah Lomu (for New Zealand, Cape Town, 18 Jun 1995)	Wing

— ANNUS MIRABILIS —

Steve Thompson and Martin Corry are the only England players ever to have made 15 appearances for their country in a calendar year, doing so in the World Cup years of 2003 and 2007 respectively – both making 13 starts and 2 replacement appearances.

Three other players in the World Cup winning team, Ben Kay, Ben Cohen and Jonny Wilkinson, started 14 England matches that year and were on the winning side every time!

The first player to top 100 test points in a calendar year for England was Rob Andrew with 113 points in eight games during 1994. Subsequently, the feat has been achieved seven times, with Jonny Wilkinson passing the 100 mark in five successive years between 1999–2003. The most points in a calendar year for England is 233 points by Jonny Wilkinson in 14 tests in 2003.

Pts	Player	Year
113	Rob Andrew	1994
132	Rob Andrew	1995
109	Paul Grayson	1998
171	Jonny Wilkinson	1999
156	Jonny Wilkinson	2000
131	Jonny Wilkinson	2001
126	Jonny Wilkinson	2002
233	Jonny Wilkinson	2003
165	Jonny Wilkinson	2007

Meanwhile, four England players have scored a record nine tries in a calendar year: Rory Underwood in 1988, Dan Luger in 1999, Will Greenwood and Josh Lewsey in 2003.

ENGLAND SHIRTS 1871 – 2009

1871 – Mar 1992

1991 World Cup

Oct 1992 – Mar 1995

1995 World Cup

Nov 1995 – Mar 1996

Nov 1996 – July 1997

Nov 1997-Aug 1999

1999 World Cup Qualifiers

26 June 1999 (v Australia)

1999 World Cup

1999 World Cup (20th Oct, v Fiji)

Feb 2000 – Oct 2001

Nov 2001 – Apr 2002

June 2002 – Sept 2003

Sept 2003 – June 2005

2003 World Cup

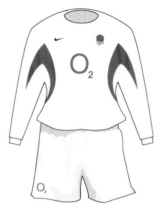

Nov 2005 – June 2007

Aug 2007 - 2009

18 August 2007 (v France)

2007 World Cup

— THE FLUSH OF YOUTH —

Harlequins fly-half Colin Laird is England's youngest ever player, being aged just 18 years 134 days when he made his debut against Wales at Twickenham in January 1927. Four weeks later, in his next international match against Ireland at Twickenham, he duly became England's youngest ever try scorer, grabbing the first of England's two tries in an 8–6 win.

The youngest ever England captain is Frederic Stokes who led his country in the very first test match against Scotland at Raeburn Place, Edinburgh on 27 March 1871. He was just 20 years and 258 days old.

— MAN AT THE HELM —

Charting the history of England coaches has been a difficult task with the changing job titles of the top man in charge at the time. For instance Clive Woodward began his seven year tenure at the helm simply as "coach", which then evolved into "Team manager" and then into "Head coach" by 2002.

It can safely be considered that England's first "coach" was Don White in 1969.

Name	Job title	1st match	Last match	P	W	D	L
Don White	Team manager	20 Dec 1969	17 Apr 1971	11	3	1	7
John Elders	National coach*	15 Jan 1972	16 Mar 1974	16	6	1	9
John Burgess	National coach*	18 Jan 1975	31 May 1975	6	1	-	5
Peter Colston	National coach*	3 Jan 1976	17 Mar 1979	18	6	1	11
Mike Davis	National coach*	24 Nov 1979	6 Mar 1982	16	10	2	4
Dick Greenwood	National coach*	15 Jan 1983	20 Apr 1985	17	4	2	11
Martin Green	National coach*	1 Jun 1985	8 Jun 1987	14	5	-	9
Geoff Cooke	Team manager	16 Jan 1988	19 Mar 1994	49	35	1	13
Jack Rowell	Team coach	4 Jun 1994	12 Jul 1997	29	21	-	8
Clive Woodward	Head coach	15 Nov 1997	2 Jun 2004	83	59	2	22
Andy Robinson	Head coach	13 Nov 2004	25 Nov 2006	22	9	-	13
Brian Ashton	Head coach	3 Feb 2007	15 Mar 2008	22	12	-	10
Rob Andrew	Team manager	14 Jun 2008	21 Jun 2008	2	-	-	2
Martin Johnson	Team manager	8 Nov 2008					

* job title unconfirmed

— LIKE FATHER, LIKE SON —

Coventry lad Ivor Preece gained a dozen caps at fly-half and centre in an England career which lasted from 1948–51, including five matches as captain. His son Peter then continued the family tradition by first following his father into the Coventry team and then into the England side, making his debut at centre on the tour to South Africa in June 1972. The gap of just 21 years between a father and son appearing in a test side is easily an England record. By a strange quirk Peter, like his father, ended up with 12 caps for his country.

— WOODWARD'S FIRST TEAM —

Clive Woodward's first match in charge of the England team was the 15–15 draw against Australia at Twickenham on 15 November 1997. The side he chose (below) contained four new caps:

No.	Name	Club	Caps
15	Matt Perry	Bath	0
14	David Rees	Sale	0
13	Will Greenwood	Leicester Tigers	0
12	Phil de Glanville	Bath	24
11	Adedayo Adebayo	Bath	3
10	Mike Catt	Bath	23
9	Kyran Bracken	Saracens	14
1	Jason Leonard	Harlequins	55
2	Andy Long	Bath	0
3	Will Green	Wasps	0
4	Martin Johnson	Leicester Tigers	30
5	Garath Archer	Newcastle	2
6	Lawrence Dallaglio (capt)	Wasps	12
7	Richard Hill	Saracens	5
8	Tony Diprose	Saracens	2

Replacements:

No.	Name	Club	Caps
16	Paul Grayson	Northampton	8
17	Austin Healey*	Leicester Tigers	3
18	Neil Back	Leicester Tigers	5
19	Danny Grewcock	Saracens	7
20	Graham Rowntree	Leicester Tigers	15
21	Richard Cockerill*	Leicester Tigers	2

*Cockerill replaced Long at half-time and Healey replaced Adebayo after 65 minutes. In addition, Paul Grayson was a blood substitute for de Glanville during the first half.

— FIRST REPLACEMENT —

England first used a replacement in an international on 15 March 1969, when Coventry wing Tim Dalton came on for Keith Fielding, who had twisted an ankle, against Scotland at Twickenham. The previous year the IRB had ruled that replacements could be used for the first time in tests but only after an independent doctor had decreed that the substituted player was unfit to continue.

Temporary replacements to cover for players who had been cut on the field of play were first introduced in 1993. England's first such 'blood bin' cap was Dewi Morris, who came on for Kyran Bracken between the 16th and 22nd minutes against Scotland at Twickenham on 18 March 1995.

Tactical substitutions were made legal for the first time by the IRB on 4 November 1996. England used three tactical subs in their very next test against Italy at Twickenham in a 54–21 victory, the first seeing Rob Hardwick, the Coventry prop, coming on for Jason Leonard after 70 minutes to win his only test cap.

— CALCUTTA CUP —

The Calcutta Club

On Christmas Day 1872, a game of rugby football between 20 players representing England and 20 representing Scotland, Ireland and Wales, was played in Calcutta.

The match was such a success that it was repeated a week later: the game of rugby had reached India and the Calcutta Football Club was formed in January 1873.

The Calcutta Club joined the Rugby Football Union in 1874. Although the Indian climate was not entirely suitable for rugby, the club prospered during its first year. However, membership predictably dropped when the club's free bar was discontinued. Meanwhile, other sports, such as tennis and polo, which were considered to be more suited to the local climate, were attracting potential members away from the rugby club. Eventually, the members decided to disband, but they left a lasting legacy. Keen to perpetuate the name of the club they withdrew the club's remaining funds from the bank in silver rupees, had them melted down and made into a cup. The trophy, known as the Calcutta Cup, was presented to the RFU in 1878 with the proviso that it should be competed for annually.

The Cup

The cup itself is of Indian workmanship, and stands approximately 18 inches (45 cm) high. The body is finely engraved with three king cobras forming the handles. The domed lid is surmounted by an elephant which, it is said, portrays one from the Viceroy's own stock and is complete with a howdah. The inscription on the cup's wooden base reads: THE CALCUTTA CUP.

Additional plates are attached to the base which record the date of each match played, the name of the winning country and the names of the two captains. There is an anomaly in the recording of the winning country on the base of the cup. It was first played for in 1879, but the plinth shows records extending back to the first international in 1871.

The original Calcutta Cup is housed at the Museum of Rugby, Twickenham, when won by England. When Scotland lift the cup a full-size replica is displayed at the museum instead. The SRU also own a replica which, like the English one, was made using modern technology.

The Competition

When they were presented with the trophy in 1878, the RFU rejected the idea of making the Calcutta Cup a knock-out competition for English club sides, believing that 'competitiveness' ran against the amateur ethos. Instead, the RFU decided that the cup would be awarded to the winners of an annual fixture between England and Scotland. The first Calcutta Cup match was played at Raeburn Place, Edinburgh, on 10 March 1879 and ended in a draw; Scotland scoring a drop goal and England a goal. The following year, on 28 February 1880, England became the first winners of the Calcutta Cup when they defeated Scotland by 2 goals and 3 tries to a single goal at Manchester.

England's longest tenure of the Calcutta Cup was for 13 years between 1951 and 1964, while Scotland's longest spell as holders was for four years between 1893 and 1897.

— THE NEW PROFESSIONALISM —

On 26 August 1995 at the Concorde Hotel in Paris the game of rugby union turned open for the first time with the IRB lifting all its restrictions on payments relating to the game of Rugby Union, thus bringing the game's amateur age to an end.

England's first match of the professional era followed on 18 November 1995 when South Africa were the visitors to a newly refurbished Twickenham (taking on it's horseshoe shape for the first time), but the Springboks spoiled the party with a 24–14 victory.

Jack Rowell selected the following as England's first 'professional' side.

England:		Club	Caps
15	Jon Callard	Bath	4
14	Damian Hopley	Wasps	1
13	Will Carling (capt)	Harlequins	60
12	Jerry Guscott	Bath	39
11	Rory Underwood	Leicester	79
10	Mike Catt	Bath	12
9	Kyran Bracken	Bristol	10
1	Jason Leonard	Harlequins	43
2	Mark Regan	Bristol*	0
3	Victor Ubogu	Bath	20
4	Martin Johnson	Leicester	18
5	Martin Bayfield	Northampton	27
6	Tim Rodber	Northampton	20
7	Andy Robinson	Bath	7
8	Ben Clarke	Bath	22
Bench:			
16	Lawrence Dallaglio	Wasps*	0
17	Phil De Glanville	Bath	13
18	David Pears	Harlequins	4
19	Matt Dawson	Northampton	0
20	Graham Rowntree	Leicester	3
21	Graham Dawe	Bath	5

* Made test debut.

Mark Regan therefore has the honour of becoming England's first professional player – the first to make his debut in the 'open era'.

England's last amateur test match had been the Rugby World Cup 3rd place match against France in Pretoria on 22 June 1995. Ian Hunter and Dewi Morris made their final England appearances in this match and so can jointly be regarded as England's final amateur players.

— ENGLAND LEGENDS: JASON LEONARD —

Jason Leonard's big international break came on England's tour of Argentina in 1990, his performance against the formidable Tucuman Province earning him the call up for his debut cap in the first test against the Pumas. He kept his place for the second test, starting what turned out to be a run of 40 consecutive international appearances.

A member of England's Five Nations Grand Slam winning sides of 1991, 1992, 1995 and Six Nations Grand Slam team of 2003, Leonard also represented his country in four World Cups. He went on to win a world record 114 caps for his country, a total since surpassed by Australia's George Gregan.

Leonard's achievements are even more remarkable in view of the career threatening injury he suffered in May 1992. He was only able to return to action after surgeons carried out an operation inserting a piece of hip bone to repair a ruptured vertebra in the top of his neck. However, such were his powers of recovery that he was back playing club rugby by October, and in the same month he represented England in the international against Canada.

Jason Leonard: 114 caps, 1 try

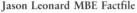

Jason Leonard MBE Factfile
Born: 14 Aug 1968 in Barking, London
Clubs: Barking, Saracens, Harlequins
Caps: 114 (W86, D2, L24)
Scoring: 1 try – 5 pts
England debut: 28 Jul 1990 vs Argentina (Buenos Aires)

— ROYALLY ENTERTAINED —

The current Royal Princes, Harry and William, are true rugby fans and can be regularly seen at rugby games at Twickenham and elsewhere. However, a royal connection with England rugby is in fact nothing new. Their grandmother, Queen Elizabeth II, handed the 1991 Rugby World Cup trophy to Australian captain Nick Farr-Jones at Twickenham following their victory over England, and is patron of the Rugby Football Union.

King George V made his first visit to Twickenham following his succession on 14 February 1914 for the visit of Ireland and had been a regular attendee when he was Prince of Wales. He also became Patron of the RFU and attended many more matches over the years, indeed both sides wore black armbands as a sign of respect when Ireland faced England at Lansdowne Road in February 1936 just over two weeks after his death at Sandringham. The England-Ireland game in 1952 was postponed for six weeks due to the death of his son King George VI and was eventually played at the end of March in a blizzard. In 1901 England and Ireland wore black armbands following the death of Queen Victoria at Osborne House the previous week.

— NEW STARTER BECOMES THE BOSS —

Four England players have marked their test debut by also captaining their country. The first player to pull off this rare double was Frederic Stokes in the very first international match against Scotland in 1871. He was followed by Frederick Alderson, twenty years later against Wales; Joe Mycock, who skippered his country on debut in England's first match following World War II; and, finally, Wasps scrum-half Nigel Melville, who led England on his debut against Australia at Twickenham in 1984.

— WHERE THERE'S A WILL —

When Will Carling first skippered England against Australia at Twickenham on 5 November 1988 he was just 22 years old and the youngest of the 15 England players in the side. Carling remained the youngest player in the team for England's next nine tests, all of which saw him lead out the side as captain. He was finally accompanied by younger players when Jason Leonard, David Pears and Dean Ryan all appeared in the first test against Argentina in 1990.

The only other England captain to be younger than all his team-mates was 23-year-old Peter Cranmer, who skippered the side against Wales in Cardiff on 15 January 1938.

— THE ACCUMULATORS —

The players who have scored an average of five points or more per cap:

Name	Tries	Conv	DG	PG	Pts	Caps	Pts/ Match
Jonny Wilkinson	6	144	29	209	1032	66+4	14.7
Simon Hodgkinson	1	35	-	43	203	14	14.5
Jon Callard	-	3	-	21	69	5	13.8
Paul Grayson	2	78	6	72	400	24+8	12.5
Grahame Parker	-	6	-	4	24	2	12.0
Dave Walder	2	11	-	3	41	3+1	10.3
Dusty Hare	2	14	1	67	240	25	9.6
Jon Webb	4	41	-	66	296	32+1	9.0
Charlie Hodgson	6	44	3	44	259	25+5	8.6
Marcus Rose	2	4	-	22	82	10	8.2
Bob Hiller	3	12	2	33	138	19	7.3
Sam Doble	-	1	-	6	20	3	6.7
Daniel Lambert	8	8	-	2	46	7	6.6
Roger Hosen	-	6	-	17	63	10	6.3
Alan Old	1	8	3	23	98	16	6.1
Howard Marshall	3	-	-	-	6	1	6.0
Danny Cipriani	-	3	-	4	18	1+2	6.0
Rob Andrew	2	33	21	86	396	69+2	5.6
Andy Goode	-	7	1	10	47	3+6	5.2

— ENGLAND LEGENDS: ROGER UTTLEY —

Blackpool-born lock Roger Uttley was a tough and robust forward blessed with a shrewd rugby brain. He earned his England spurs as a 23-year-old in 1973, two years after touring the Far East where he played in five 'non-capped tests' against Japan (2), Singapore and Sri Lanka (2).

A fixture in the England team for most of the 1970s, Uttley was a versatile player who gained 11 caps in the second row, seven caps at number 8 and the remaining five on the blindside flank. Skipper in seven tests, he eventually retired from playing in 1980 after helping England to their first Grand Slam in 23 years, achieved with a famous 30–18 win over Scotland.

Uttley, who was a school master at Harrow, later carved out an impressive career as coach. In 1991 he guided the national team to the Grand Slam, thus becoming the first Englishman to win a slam as a player and a coach. He was rewarded for his achievement by being awarded the OBE later that year.

Roger Miles Uttley OBE Factfile
Born: 11 Sep 1949 in Blackpool, Lancashire
Clubs: Gosforth, Wasps
Caps: 23 (W12, D2, L9)
Scoring: 2 tries − 8 pts
England debut: 10 Feb 1973 vs Ireland (Dublin)

— ENGLAND AT THE THIRD RUGBY WORLD CUP: 1995 —

Games and Scorers:
Pool B

27 May	Argentina	Durban	W 24–18	p: Andrew 6. d: Andrew 2	
31 May	Italy	Durban	W 27–20	t: T.Underwood, R.Underwood. c: Andrew. p: Andrew 5	
4 June	W Samoa	Durban	W 44–22	t: R.Underwood 2, Back. c: Callard 3. p: Callard 5	

RWC Pool B Table:

Nation	P	W	D	L	F	A	Pts	Tries
England	3	3	0	0	95	60	9	6
Western Samoa	3	2	0	1	96	88	7	12
Italy	3	1	0	2	69	94	5	7
Argentina	3	0	0	3	69	87	3	8

Quarter-final

11 June	Australia	Cape Town	W 25–22	t: T.Underwood. c: Andrew. p: Andrew 5. d: Andrew

Semi-final

18 June	N Zealand	Cape Town	L 29–45	t: R.Underwood 2, Carling 2. c: Andrew 3. p: Andrew

3rd Place Playoff

22 June	France	Pretoria	L 9–19	p: Andrew 3

Squad and Appearances:

Manager: Jack Rowell. Coach: Les Cusworth. Captain: Will Carling.
Rob Andrew (Wasps) Ar/It/Au/NZ/F; Neil Back (Leicester Tigers)
Ar(r)/It/Sm; Martin Bayfield (Northampton Saints) Ar/It/Au/NZ/F;
Kyran Bracken (Bristol) It/Sm(r); Jon Callard (Bath) Sm; Will Carling
(Harlequins) Ar/Sm/Au/NZ/F; Mike Catt (Bath) Ar/It/Sm/Au/NZ/F;
Ben Clarke (Bath) Ar/It/Au/NZ/F; Graham Dawe (Bath) Sm; Phil De
Glanville (Bath) Ar(r)/It/Sm; Andy Gomarsall (Wasps)*; Jerry Guscott
(Bath) Ar/It/Au/NZ/F; Damian Hopley (Wasps) Sm(r); Ian Hunter
(Northampton Saints) Sm/F; Martin Johnson (Leicester Tigers)
Ar/It/Sm/Au/NZ/F; Jason Leonard (Harlequins) Ar/It/Au/NZ/F;
John Mallett (Bath) Sm(r); Brian Moore (Harlequins) Ar/It/Sm(r)/
Au/NZ/F; Dewi Morris (Orrell) Ar/Sm/Au/NZ/F; Steve Ojomoh
(Bath) Ar/Sm/Au(r)/F; Dean Richards (Leicester Tigers) Sm/Au/NZ;
Tim Rodber (Northampton Saints) Ar/It/Sm(r)/Au/NZ/F; Graham
Rowntree (Leicester Tigers) It/Sm; Victor Ubogu (Bath) Ar/Sm/
Au/NZ/F; Rory Underwood (Leicester Tigers) Ar/It/Sm/Au/NZ/F; Tony
Underwood (Leicester Tigers) Ar/It/Au/NZ; Richard West (Gloucester)
Sm.

Rob Andrew was captain against Italy. Appearances as a
replacement marked with (r).

* Due to injuries, Gomarsall was a late inclusion.

Scoring:

Name	T	C	P	D	Pts
Rob Andrew	-	5	20	3	79
Rory Underwood	5	-	-	-	25
Jon Callard	-	3	5	-	21
Will Carling	2	-	-	-	10
Tony Underwood	2	-	-	-	10
Neil Back	1	-	-	-	5
Penalty Try	1	-	-	-	5
Mike Catt	-	-	-	1	3
TOTALS	11	8	25	4	158
AGAINST	16	9	14	2	146

— ENGLAND LEGENDS: FRAN COTTON —

Fran Cotton was a genuine world-class prop, being especially effective on either side of the scrum due to his immense strength and size. Hailing from a rugby league background (his father and brother both turned out for Warrington), Cotton first played club rugby with Liverpool but it was while he was studying at Loughborough that he came to prominence.

As captain of the North-West Counties team which defeated New Zealand at the Ellis Sports Ground, Workington on 22 November 1972, Cotton became the first ever skipper of a non-international English team to beat an All Black team. His experiences leading his country were less successful, skippering England to three losses in the Five Nations Championship in 1975.

Off the field, Cotton set up a kit manufacturing company, Cotton Traders, which at one time supplied kit to half of the world's top national sides.

Francis Edward Cotton Factfile
Born: 3 Jan 1948 in Wigan, Lancashire
Clubs: Liverpool, Coventry, Sale
Caps: 31 (W13, L18)
Scoring: 1 try – 4 pts
England debut: 20 Mar 1971 vs Scotland (Twickenham)

— DAD'S ARMY —

The England team at the 2003 Rugby World Cup in Australia was tagged 'Dad's Army' by the local media because of the inclusion of some long-in-the-tooth veterans in the squad. However, the tag was a little cruel as the side was actually younger than the one which competed in the 1991 World Cup final against Australia at Twickenham. In England's 580 test matches to date this is oldest XV to take to the field, with an average age of just over 30.

The 1991 'oldies' lined up as follows: Jon Webb (aged 28); Simon Halliday (31), Will Carling (25), Jeremy Guscott (26), Rory Underwood (28); Rob Andrew (28), Richard Hill (30); Jason Leonard (23), Brian Moore (29), Jeff Probyn (35); Wade Dooley (34), Paul Ackford (33); Mickey Skinner (32), Mike Teague (32) and Peter Winterbottom (31).

— CLOSE ENCOUNTERS OF THE ONE POINT KIND: WINS —

Date	Result	Venue
17 Jan 1914	England 10, Wales 9	Twickenham
21 Mar 1914	Scotland 15, England 16	Inverleith
11 Feb 1928	Ireland 6, England 7	Dublin
21 Mar 1936	England 9, Scotland 8	Twickenham
16 Jan 1937	England 4, Wales 3	Twickenham
13 Feb 1937	England 9, Ireland 8	Twickenham
23 Feb 1963	England 6, France 5	Twickenham
15 Mar 1975	England 7, Scotland 6	Twickenham
3 Mar 1979	England 7, France 6	Twickenham
16 Feb 1980	England 9, Wales 8	Twickenham
16 Jan 1993	England 16, France 15	Twickenham
5 Feb 1994	Scotland 14, England 15	Murrayfield
16 Nov 2002	England 32, Australia 31	Twickenham

— CLOSE ENCOUNTERS OF THE ONE POINT KIND: DEFEATS —

Date	Result	Venue
7 Jan 1893	Wales 12, England 11	Cardiff
11 Jan 1902	England 8, Wales 9	Blackheath
9 Feb 1929	England 5, Ireland 6	Twickenham
8 Feb 1930	Ireland 4, England 3	Dublin
14 Feb 1931	England 5, Ireland 6	Twickenham
6 Apr 1931	France 14, England 13	Paris
14 Feb 1948	England 10, Ireland 11	Twickenham
20 Mar 1971	England 15, Scotland 16	Twickenham
6 Mar 1976	England 12, Ireland 13	Twickenham
19 Feb 1977	England 3, France 4	Twickenham
24 Nov 1979	England 9, New Zealand 10	Twickenham
6 Feb 1982	England 15, Ireland 16	Twickenham
16 Jan 1988	France 10, England 9	Paris
6 Feb 1993	Wales 10, England 9	Cardiff
19 Feb 1994	England 12, Ireland 13	Twickenham
28 Nov 1998	England 11, Australia 12	Twickenham
11 Apr 1999	Wales 32, England 31	Wembley
30 Aug 2003	France 17, England 16	Marseille
13 Feb 2005	England 17, France 18	Twickenham

— A LATE DEVELOPER —

Devonport Services full-back Frederick Gilbert was very nearly 39 years of age when he was first picked for England for the match against Wales at Twickenham on 20 January 1923 (Gilbert's actual birthdate has never been established but his birth was registered in Plymouth during the 'March quarter' of 1884). Three weeks later he kept his place for the visit of Ireland to Welford Road, Leicester, in what was to be his final test appearance. Although his exact age isn't known, Gilbert remains England's oldest ever test player.

England's oldest try scorer is Sale hooker Eric Evans who crossed the line against France at Twickenham in 1957 aged 36 years and 22 days.

Evans is also England's oldest ever captain, who was almost 38 when he led England for the final time against Scotland at Murrayfield in 1958.

— BILLY WILLIAMS'S CABBAGE PATCH —

The site of the famous Twickenham ground was originally purchased by the RFU for £5,572 12s 6d during the 1907–08 season. Two men played a key role in obtaining the site, which had previously been a cabbage field, for the organisation: William Cail, RFU treasurer, handled the financial side of the deal; while Billy Williams, a member of the RFU committee, took the credit for the discovery of the field. 'Billy Williams's cabbage patch' soon became headquarters of the RFU, and the first England match was played at the new venue on 15 January 1910. England got off to a good start, too, with a 11–6 win over Wales.

However, critics still lambasted the RFU for choosing to make Twickenham its home. In 1912 the rugby correspondent of *The Times* described the then "picturesque village" as, "the somewhat remote and inaccessible theatre of warfare."

Crowds grew steadily from the 17,000 that watched the first game, and by 1932, when the North and West stands had been built and a second tier added to the East stand, the ground could hold 72,500 spectators, almost half of whom were seated. The new South stand was completed in 1981, and by 1995 the West, East and North stands had been rebuilt at a cost of £30 million to form a distinctive horseshoe-shaped stadium. During 2006 the South stand was levelled and rebuilt to complete today's uniform bowl-shaped ground.

Twickenham records and curiosities:
Jason Leonard is the only player to have appeared in over 50 test matches at Twickenham, his tally being 55 between 1990 and 2004.

The top try scorer at HQ is Rory Underwood with 27 tries in 41 appearances between 1984 and 1996.

The top points scorer is Jonny Wilkinson, who has scored 7 tries, 95 conversions, 108 penalty goals and 9 drop goals for a massive total of 576 points for England at Twickenham. In all that time Jonny missed just 44 kicks at goal at the ground (24 conversions and 20 penalties) for a phenomenal 83% kicking success rate at HQ.

The most matches without defeat at Twickenham is eleven by Dewi Morris (ten wins and a draw), while the best 100% winning records belong to Dorian West and Nick Beal, who won eight games apiece at HQ.

Peter Wheeler was on the losing side at Twickenham more than any other player (12 defeats in 24 capped matches).

Dean Ryan, Dave Walder and David Pears all gained four caps for England, but never turned out for their country at Twickenham.

Twickenham before re-development began in 1981

— TWO OLD TO PLAY —

Brothers Chris and Alan Old twice turned out for England on the same day, Chris playing cricket and Alan rugby. On 2 February 1974 Alan scored a penalty goal in the 14–16 loss to Scotland at Murrayfield, while Chris hit 11 runs batting for England on the first day of the First test against the West Indies in Port-of-Spain, Trinidad. Two weeks later Alan scored 17 points in England's 21–26 loss to Ireland at Twickenham; meanwhile, younger brother Chris watched from the pavilion in Kingston, Jamaica as England ended the day on 251–5.

— BIRTHDAY BOYS —

Seventeen players have turned out for England on their birthday, Rob Andrew and Will Greenwood doing so twice:

Date	Name	Opponent	Venue	Age
13 Feb 1932	John Hodgson	Ireland	Lansdowne Road	23
17 Jan 1948	David Swarbrick	Wales	Twickenham	21
19 Mar 1949	Clive Van Ryneveld	Scotland	Twickenham	21
25 Feb 1950	Brian Boobbyer	France	Paris	22
18 Jan 1958	Peter Thompson	Wales	Twickenham	29
1 Feb 1958	Eric Evans	Australia	Twickenham	37
3 Jan 1976	Fran Cotton	Australia	Twickenham	29
24 Nov 1979	John Carleton	New Zealand	Twickenham	24
5 Mar 1983	Colin Smart	Scotland	Twickenham	33
18 Feb 1989	Rob Andrew	Ireland	Lansdowne Road	26
18 Feb 1989	Paul Rendall	Ireland	Lansdowne Road	35
8 Oct 1991	Mike Teague	Italy	Twickenham	32
18 Feb 1995	Rob Andrew	Wales	Cardiff	32
22 Nov 1997	Kyran Bracken	New Zealand	Manchester	26
20 Oct 1999	Will Greenwood	Fiji	Twickenham	27
20 Oct 2001	Will Greenwood	Ireland	Lansdowne Road	29
14 Jun 2003	Joe Worsley	New Zealand	Wellington	26
18 Oct 2003	Mike Tindall	South Africa	Perth	25
12 Nov 2005	Charlie Hodgson	Australia	Twickenham	25

Eric Evans is the only player to have captained England on his birthday. Joe Worsley is the only player to have come off the replacements bench on his birthday.

Just two players have scored tries on their birthday: Clive van Ryneveld (2) and Peter Thompson (1).

Two others have scored points on their birthday: Rob Andrew (8 points) in 1989 and 1995, and Charlie Hodgson (11 points) in 2005.

John Carleton is the only England player to make his test debut on his birthday.

Bristol's Jason Hobson was an unused replacement against Italy in Rome on 10 Feb 2008. It was his 25th birthday.

— QUICK DEBUT TRIES —

The fastest England try on debut was scored by Fred Chapman against Wales in the first ever test match played at Twickenham on 15 January 1910. The speedy Westoe wing touched down after just 75 seconds, nearly two minutes faster than the previous record set by Edgar Mobbs on his debut against Australia a year earlier.

Name	Timing	Opponent (Venue)	Date
Fred Chapman	75 seconds	v Wales (Twickenham)	15 Jan 1910
Edgar Mobbs	3 minutes	v Australia (Blackheath)	9 Jan 1909
Herbert Gardner	5 minutes	v Ireland (Dublin)	11 Mar 1878
John Smith	5 minutes	v Wales (Twickenham)	21 Jan 1950
Alex Sanderson*	6 minutes	v Romania (Twickenham)	17 Nov 2001
Nick Greenstock	7 minutes	v Argentina (Buenos Aires)	31 May 1997
Bill Perry	10 minutes	v Ireland (Dublin)	11 Mar 1878
Hugh Vyvyan*	10 minutes	v Canada (Twickenham)	13 Nov 2004

* Replacement players

Rob Andrew holds the record for the fastest score by an England debut player, dropping a goal against Romania after just 47 seconds in January 1985.

— SOUTH SEA ISLAND VOLCANO —

The first south sea islander to play for England was ex-New Zealand rugby league international wing Lesley Vainikolo against Wales at Twickenham on 2 February 2008.

The "Volcano" was born in Nuku'alofa, Tonga in May 1979 and first appeared for the Canberra Raiders in Australian rugby league's NRL competition in 1998. The following year he won the first of eight league caps for the Kiwis, before transferring over to the Bradford Bulls in 2002. He signed for Gloucester in the summer of 2007 and scored five tries on his union debut in the Guinness Premiership at Leeds before being "fast tracked" by the England management, making his test debut after just ten games in the code.

— ENGLAND LEGENDS: ERIC EVANS —

Sale front-rower Eric Evans began his England career playing out of position at loosehead prop against Australia in 1948. A second cap followed two years later against Wales in his usual position of hooker, but it wasn't until 1951 that he became an international regular.

Having led Lancashire to victory in the 1948 County Championship final against Eastern Counties at Cambridge, Evans graduated to the England captaincy in 1956. A year later he skippered his country to their first Grand Slam since 1928, an achievement followed by a momentous victory over the touring Wallabies in 1958.

Evans became England's most capped hooker in 1958 and held this record until overtaken by John Pullin in 1973.

Eric Evans Factfile
Born: 1 Feb 1921 in Droylsden, Manchester
Club: Sale
Caps: 30 (W17, D3, L10)
Scoring: 5 tries – 15 pts
England debut: 3 Jan 1948 vs Australia (Twickenham)

— IN POSITION —

The most test match appearances for England in the key playing positions:

Full-back	Matt Perry	35*	1997–2001
Wing	Rory Underwood	85	1984–1996
Centre	Will Carling	72	1988–1997
Fly-half	Rob Andrew	70**	1985–1997
Scrum-half	Matt Dawson	77	1995–2006
Prop	Jason Leonard	114	1990–2004
Hooker	Brian Moore	64	1987–1995
Lock	Martin Johnson	84	1993–2003
Flanker	Neil Back	66	1994–2003
No 8	Dean Richards	48	1986–1996

* Matt Perry also played one match at centre
** Rob Andrew also played one game at full-back

— TIGERS, TIGERS EVERYWHERE —

Including replacements, the record number of England caps awarded to players of one club for a single international is nine, when Leicester Tigers provided five members of the starting line-up (including the captain) and four others came off the bench against Canada at Twickenham on 28 August 1999:

No:	Name	Club
15	Matt Perry	Bath
14	Dan Luger	Saracens
13	**Will Greenwood**	**Leicester Tigers**
12	Jeremy Guscott	Bath
11	**Austin Healey**	**Leicester Tigers**
10	Jonny Wilkinson	Newcastle Falcons
9	Matt Dawson	Northampton Saints
1	**Graham Rowntree**	**Leicester Tigers**
2	Phil Greening	Sale
3	Phil Vickery	Gloucester
4	**Martin Johnson (capt)**	**Leicester Tigers**
5	Danny Grewcock	Saracens
6	Richard Hill	Saracens
7	**Neil Back**	**Leicester Tigers**
8	Lawrence Dallaglio	London Wasps

Replacements:

16	**Tim Stimpson**	**Leicester Tigers**	**for Perry 59'**
17	Mike Catt	Bath	for Guscott 73'
18	Nick Beal	Northampton Saints	for Healey 50'
19	**Martin Corry**	**Leicester Tigers**	**for Johnson 7'–14'**
20	**Darren Garforth**	**Leicester Tigers**	**for Vickery 50'**
21	Jason Leonard	Harlequins	for Rowntree 50'
22	**Richard Cockerill**	**Leicester Tigers**	**for Greening 50'**

On four other occasions Leicester have had eight players capped for England on the same day.

— FORWARD OR BACK —

Hugh Campbell Rowley holds a unique place in the history of England rugby as the only player to start a test both as a forward and as a back.

Rowley began his England career as a forward against Scotland at Raeburn Place, Edinburgh in 1879 and won six caps in the pack before switching to half-back (in those days the fly-half and scrum-half roles were interchangeable) for two games in 1881 and 1882. In his final test appearance against Scotland at Manchester in 1882, he reverted to playing as a forward.

— 4,000 MINUTES WITHOUT A TRY —

The only England international to have played for over 4,000 minutes without scoring a try is durable prop Jason Leonard and, curiously, he has achieved the feat twice.

In an incredible career during which he amassed a then world record 114 caps for his country, Leonard crossed for just one test try, in the 72nd minute of his only match as England captain against Argentina at Twickenham on 14 December 1996. Amazingly, taking the total playing time he accumulated in an England shirt (8,124 minutes), Leonard's single try came almost exactly in the middle of his test career. His big moment came in the 4,049th minute, after which he failed to score again in the remaining 4,075 minutes he played for England.

— ENGLAND LEGENDS: 'DAVE' DAVIES —

Of his 22 appearances for England, W.J.A. Davies only lost one – his international debut against South Africa in 1913. Few players, before or since, can boast such an impressive record.

Davies was England's most capped fly-half for 67 years until he was overtaken by Rob Andrew in 1989. He established a record half-back partnership with Royal Navy team-mate Cecil Kershaw, the pair being known as 'Dave and K.'. Davies was renowned as one of the first tactical kickers in the game, and was as adept at dropping left-footed goals as he was kicking from the hand.

During World War I, he served aboard HMS *Iron Duke* and HMS *Queen Elizabeth*, and in 1919 was awarded an OBE for his efforts on the staff of the commander of the fleet at Jutland.

After hostilities ceased, Davies returned to international rugby, skippering England to two Grand Slam titles in 1921 and 1923.

William John Abbott Davies OBE Factfile
Born: 21 Jun 1890 in Pembroke, Wales
Clubs: United Services, Royal Navy, Combined Services
Caps: 22 (W20, D1, L1)
Scoring: 4T, 3DG – 24 pts
England debut: 4 Jan 1913 vs South Africa (Twickenham)

— SURRENDERING A LEAD —

England's worst loss of a lead came in the last quarter against France at Twickenham on 1 March 1997. Paul Grayson's fourth penalty goal in the 51st minute gave England a comfortable-looking 20–6, but ten minutes later Laurent Leflamand's try kick-started an amazing fightback which saw France score 17 unanswered points to win 23–20. The greatest leads surrendered by England are:

Pts	Score	Result	Venue	Date
14	England 20, France 6 (51mins)	Lost 20–23	Twickenham	1 Mar 1997
13	England 19, Wales 6 (57 mins)	Lost 19–26	Twickenham	2 Feb 2008
11	England 11, South Africa 0 (11 mins)	Lost 11–29	Twickenham	29 Nov 1997
11	England 17, France 6 (36 mins)	Lost 17–18	Twickenham	13 Feb 2005
10	England 13, Wales 3 (1st half)	Lost 13–17	Twickenham	28 Feb 1970
10	England 13, Australia 3 (22 mins)	Lost 16–22	Brisbane	29 May 1988
10	England 25, Wales 15 (39 mins)	Lost 31–32	Wembley	11 Apr 1999

And to draw:

14	England 20, New Zealand 6 (31 mins)	Drew 26–26	Twickenham	6 Dec 1997

— TWO FINGERS FOR ENGLAND —

Colin White of Gosforth lost three fingers in a forestry accident in 1978, but his disability didn't prevent him from making his England debut five years later at the age of 34. He went on to win four England caps at loosehead prop in successive matches in 1983–84.

James Hutchinson also overcame a problem with his hand, following a childhood accident with a harvesting machine, to win a cap against Ireland in 1906.

— COMEBACK KINGS —

The biggest deficit England have overturned to win a test is 12 points. England were losing 19–31 after 56 minutes against Australia at Twickenham on 16 Nov 2002, but went on to win 32–31, thanks to the ever-reliable boot of Jonny Wilkinson and a 67th minute try by Ben Cohen.

Greatest deficits turned around to win:

Pts	Score	Result	Venue	Date
12	England 19, Australia 31 (56 mins)	Won 32–31	Twickenham	16 Nov 2002
11	England 0, Ireland 11 (50 mins)	Won 14–11	Dublin	14 Feb 1920
10	England 0, Samoa 10 (8 mins)	Won 35–22	Melbourne	26 Oct 2003

— GREATEST EVER RADIO COMMENTARY —

In 2004 the BBC asked visitors to their website to nominate the greatest sports radio broadcast of all time.

A light-hearted Jon Agnew and Brian Johnston cricket commentary from 1991 won the poll, followed closely by Ian Robertson's immortal words from the nerve jangling final minutes of the 2003 Rugby World Cup final in Sydney:

"35 seconds to go. This is the one. He drops for World Cup glory . . . It's up! It's over! He's done it! Jonny Wilkinson is England's hero yet again . . ."

In the background Jonny's mentor, boss at Newcastle Falcons and ex-England fly-half Rob Andrew can be heard shrieking in ecstasy. Well, it *was* quite a moment!

"It's up! It's over!"

— ENGLAND LEGENDS: LAWRENCE DALLAGLIO —

Lawrence of England

A loyal servant to London Wasps and England, Lawrence Dallaglio achieved virtually everything an England player can. He won the 2003 Rugby World Cup and 1993 Rugby World Cup Sevens, he celebrated three Six Nations Championships (including the 2003 Grand Slam) and one Five Nations win, toured three times with the British and Irish Lions (including the victorious trip to South Africa in 1997) and captained his country 22 times.

He played in every game of the 2003 World Cup and will be remembered as part of possibly the greatest England back row (alongside Neil Back and Richard Hill) ever to play the game. He was a tremendous motivator and talisman and came out of international retirement in 2006 to help England eventually reach the Final of the 2007 World Cup.

He became Wasps' youngest captain at the age of 23 and led them to five championships and two Heineken Cup titles and briefly came out of retirement in 2008 to captain the Help For Heroes XV at Twickenham.

Lawrence Bruno Nero Dallaglio OBE Factfile
Born: 10 August 1972 in Shepherds Bush, London
Club: London Wasps
Caps: 85 (W60, D2, L23)
Scoring: 17 tries – 85 points
England debut: 18 Nov 1995 vs South Africa (Twickenham)

— NO CAP FOR UNLUCKY NORMAN —

Bath forward Norman Matthews came within just five minutes of gaining his one and only England cap on 18 January 1930 in Cardiff. Bristol's Sam Tucker had been named in the team after the original hooker, Exeter's Henry Rew dropped out on the morning of the match failing to recover from a training ground injury. However, Tucker's call up came too late for the latest train before kick-off from Bristol to Cardiff, so he instigated a franctic dash to the game involving a light aircraft and hitch hiking in a lorry. Travelling reserve Matthews stepped in and even posed for the traditional team photograph before Tucker finally showed up just five minutes before kick-off. Poor Matthews never gained that elusive England cap.

A decade before a similar incident had occurred when the Birkenhead Park wing Wilfrid Lowry was included in the official photograph just before kickoff for England's visit to Swansea in 1920. However, the selectors made a last minute change and replaced him with Leicester's Harold Day as the felt that conditions were more suited to Day's style of rugby. Lowry did not have to wait long for his first cap which he gained two weeks later against France at Twickenham.

— THE TEAM THAT NEVER WAS —

In seasons 1888 and 1889 England refused to play in the Four Nations Championship because of a long-running dispute about the award of a controversial try in the 1884 England-Scotland match at Blackheath.

In 1888 the RFU took the unusual step of announcing a team that would have played in the Championship that year and even awarded caps to its members. However, as the team never actually played a match the caps are excluded from England's official list. Seven of the team were uncapped at the time but five of these players eventually went on to wear England colours. Two unfortunate players, though, were destined never to pull on an England jersey. They were Percy Robertshaw, a Bradford three-quarter whose brother Rawson had been capped on five occasions between 1886 and 1887, and Salford forward Harry Eagles, who at least toured with the forerunners of the British and Irish Lions to Australia and New Zealand towards the end of 1888.

— ST GEORGE'S DAY —

Four England internationals were born on St George's Day, April 23rd. Basil Hill in 1880, David Hazell in 1931 (who revelled in the middle name 'St George'), Martin Cooper in 1948 and John Olver and 1961

— TEN MINUTES OF FAME —

The shortest test careers of England players:

Minutes	Name	Opponent (Venue)	Date
5 mins	Paul Hodgson	Scotland (Murrayfield)	8 Mar 2008*
6 mins	Nick Walshe	Australia (Sydney/ Melbourne)	Jun 2006*
6 mins	Matt Cairns	South Africa (Bloemfontein)	26 May 2007*
7 mins	Jason Hobson	New Zealand (Christchurch)	21 Jun 2008*
8 mins	Nick Martin	France (Paris)	26 Feb 1972
8 mins	Stuart Potter	Australia (Brisbane)	6 Jun 1998
8 mins	David Paice	N Zealand (Auckland/Christchurch)	June 2008*
9 mins	Mark van Gisbergen	Australia (Twickenham)	12 Nov 2005*
10 mins	Rob Hardwick	Italy (Twickenham)	23 Nov 1996
13 mins	Hugh Vyvyan	Canada (Twickenham)	13 Nov 2004*
14 mins	Dominic Chapman	Australia (Brisbane)	6 Jun 1998

* Still playing professional rugby as of summer 2008.

The appearances of Potter and Van Gisbergen were both as a temporary blood replacement. Nick Walshe's total spans two caps, whilst Hugh Vyvyan even found time to score a try.

The shortest career of anyone that has started a test is 53 minutes by Andy Long who was substituted at half-time of his debut match against Australia at Twickenham on 15 November 1997, came on for a brief period again as a blood replacement during the second half and then was a replacement for the last eleven minutes in his only other cap against USA in San Francisco in June 2001.

— MR DURABILITY —

The seven longest England test careers:

Timespan	Name	Tests	Debut	Last test
13 years, 202 days	Jason Leonard	114	28 Jul 1990	15 Feb 2004
12 years, 363 days	Mike Catt	69	19 Mar 1994	17 Mar 2007
12 years, 251 days	Nigel Redman	20	3 Nov 1984	12 Jul 1997
12 years, 250 days	Gary Pearce	36	3 Feb 1979	11 Oct 1991
12 years, 90 days	John Heaton	9	19 Jan 1935	19 Apr 1947
12 years, 69 days	Rob Andrew	71	5 Jan 1985	15 Mar 1997
12 years, 26 days	Rory Underwood	85	18 Feb 1984	16 Mar 1996

— FORTRESS TWICKENHAM —

When New Zealand beat France in Wellington on 9 June 2007 they eclipsed England's previous record of 22 consecutive home wins.

England's purple patch at the cabbage patch started against Tonga on 15 October 1999 and ended with a loss to Ireland on 6 March 2003. In between these dates they beat twelve different teams at HQ, including three wins against each of Australia, South Africa and France.

— UNLUCKY HOOKERS —

Sale hooker Andy Simpson must be the unluckiest player never to gain an England cap. Simpson pulled on an England replacements jersey no fewer than 18 times between 1981 and 1986, as understudy to Peter Wheeler, Steve Mills and Steve Brain, but didn't make a single appearance on the pitch.

Simpson did play six times for England on tour in Argentina and New Zealand and he also featured in an England XV in a non-cap match in Rome's Olympic Stadium in May 1986 – a game for which the Azzuri awarded caps!

Jon Raphael was almost as unfortunate as Simpson, warming the bench in 15 tests, behind first choice number 2s Peter Wheeler and John Pullin between 1975 and 79.

— THE SPLINTER BRIGADE —

No England player has sat out as many games on the replacements bench without getting his boots dirty as hooker Graham Dawe. He was an unused replacement for 33 matches between 1987 and 1996, but at least he did win five caps along the way. Another hooker, John Olver, was a nonplaying sub in 31 matches, while Graham Rowntree had 25 complete games on the bench.

Rowntree made seven appearances coming off the bench, for a record total of 32 selections as a replacement. The only other England player who has been selected as many times as a bench replacement is Martin Corry, winning 21 caps that way and sitting out another 13 complete games on the bench.

— YOU'RE NICKED —

England internationals who were, at one time or another, policemen:

Paul Ackford
Edward Barrett
Martin Bayfield
John Bentley
Mike Coulman
Wade Dooley
John Fidler
Charles Gummer
Nigel Heslop
Nigel Horton
Mark Linnett
Geoff Old
Dean Richards
George Vickery
Dorian West
W. Whiteley
Tug Wilson
John Wright.

— LONG TIME BETWEEN MEALS —

The England players who had to wait the longest time between caps:

Timespan	Name	From	To
9 years, 353 days	Kevin Yates	7 Jun 1997	26 May 2007
9 years, 44 days	John Bentley	29 May 1988	12 Sep 1997
8 years, 313 days	John Robinson	4 Mar 1893	11 Jan 1902
8 years, 291 days	Tommy Kemp	18 Mar 1939	3 Jan 1948
8 years, 277 days	John Williams	14 Apr 1956	16 Jan 1965
8 years, 74 days	Frank Sykes	19 Mar 1955	1 Jun 1963
8 years, 5 days	Graeme Dawe	30 May 1987	4 Jun 1995

— NO CHANGE —

England have never picked an unchanged team for five successive matches. They have, however, selected the same 15 players for four consecutive tests on three separate occasions, each of them during a winning Five Nations Championship campaign:

February–March 1960	February–March 1991	February–March 1995
Wales (won 14–6)	*Wales (won 25–6)*	*Ireland (won 20–8)*
Ireland (won 8–5)	*Scotland (won 21–12)*	*France (won 31–10)*
France (drew 3–3)	*Ireland (won 16–7)*	*Wales (won 23–9)*
Scotland (won 21–12)	*France (won 21–19)*	*Scotland (won 24–12)*
Don Rutherford	Simon Hodgkinson	Mike Catt
John Young	Nigel Heslop	Tony Underwood
Malcolm Phillips	Will Carling (capt)	Will Carling (capt)
Mike Weston	Jerry Guscott	Jerry Guscott
James Roberts	Rory Underwood	Rory Underwood
Richard Sharp	Rob Andrew	Rob Andrew
Dickie Jeeps (capt)	Richard Hill	Kyran Bracken
Ron Jacobs	Jason Leonard	Jason Leonard
Stanley Hodgson	Brian Moore	Brian Moore
Peter Wright	Jeff Probyn	Victor Ubogu
David Marques	Wade Dooley	Martin Johnson
John Currie	Paul Ackford	Martin Bayfield
Peter Robbins	Mike Teague	Tim Rodber
Ronald Syrett	Peter Winterbottom	Ben Clarke
William Morgan	Dean Richards	Dean Richards

— THE TALE OF TWO PAULS —

In the past 90 years the only two English players born on the same day were Paul Ackford and Paul Dodge. Both were born on Wednesday, 26 February 1958, Ackford in Hanover, West Germany, and Dodge in Leicester.

Strangely, although Dodge won 32 caps and Ackford 22, they were not even close to appearing in the same England team together. Leicester centre Dodge was an early developer, making his debut in 1978 at the age of 20 and playing until his last test in 1985. Harlequin lock Ackford, on the other hand, didn't make his international bow until 1988 at the age of 30.

— DOBBO'S GRISLY END —

Denys Douglas Dobson, who was born in 1880 and gained six caps as a forward for England in 1902–03, holds the unenviable record of being the first international to be sent off. Dobson was dismissed on 6 July for directing 'obscene language' at the referee during England's match with the Combined Northern Districts in Newcastle, New South Wales. He was suspended for eight months. Ten years later Dobson met a grisly end when, after moving to a farm in Ngama, Nyasaland (now Malawi) in central Africa, a charging rhinoceros trampled him to death.

— LION TAMERS —

Since World War II five Englishmen have been selected to tour with the British & Irish Lions before they were capped for England.

Of this quintet, Dickie Jeeps and Bill Patterson were capped for the Lions in test rugby before they were capped for England. John Brown of the RAF and Blackheath played five games on tour but was never capped for his country; Nigel Melville toured with the Lions but did not play test rugby for them; while Will Greenwood didn't make his test debut for the Lions until the 2005 tour of New Zealand – his third successive Lions tour.

Name	Club	Lions tour	England debut
Dickie Jeeps	Northampton	1955 to South Africa	21 Jan 56
Bill Patterson	Sale	1959 to Australia & New Zealand	7 Jan 61
John Brown	Blackheath	1962 to South Africa	-

| Nigel Melville | Wasps | 1983 to New Zealand | 3 Nov 84 |
| Will Greenwood | Leicester | 1997 to South Africa | 15 Nov 97 |

— WIN, WIN, WIN AGAIN —

England's best ever winning streak is 14 successive victories. The sequence began on 23 March 2002 with a 50–10 thrashing of Wales at Twickenham in the Six Nations Championship, and lasted until a 17–16 defeat by France at Marseille on 30 August 2003 in a World Cup warm-up match.

No	Date	Opponent	Venue	Result	Tournament
1	23 Mar 2002	Wales	Twickenham	Won 50–10	Six Nations
2	7 Apr 2002	Italy	Rome	Won 45–9	Six Nations
3	22 Jun 2002	Argentina	Buenos Aires	Won 26–18	
4	9 Nov 2002	New Zealand	Twickenham	Won 31–28	
5	16 Nov 2002	Australia	Twickenham	Won 32–31	
6	23 Nov 2002	South Africa	Twickenham	Won 53–3	
7	15 Feb 2003	France	Twickenham	Won 25–17	Six Nations
8	22 Feb 2003	Wales	Cardiff	Won 26–9	Six Nations
9	9 Mar 2003	Italy	Twickenham	Won 40–5	Six Nations
10	22 Mar 2003	Scotland	Twickenham	Won 40–9	Six Nations
11	30 Mar 2003	Ireland	Dublin	Won 42–6	Six Nations
12	14 Jun 2003	New Zealand	Wellington	Won 15–13	
13	21 Jun 2003	Australia	Melbourne	Won 25–14	
14	23 Aug 2003	Wales	Cardiff	Won 43–9	

— LOSE, LOSE, LOSE AGAIN —

England's worst ever losing run is seven defeats in a row, recorded three times: firstly between a 3–6 loss to Scotland at Inverleith on 19 March 1904 until they won 9–3 against Scotland at Inverleith on 17 March 1906. This sequence was equalled in a run started with a 15–16 defeat to Scotland at Twickenham on 20 Mar 1971 and ended with an 18–9 victory against South Africa at Ellis Park, Johannesburg on 3 June 1972. Finally, the most recent losing run began with a 12–18 loss to Scotland at Murrayfield on 25 February 2006 and ended with a 23–21 victory over South Africa at Twickenham on 18 November 2006.

— SLAM FLUNK! —

The games when England had a chance of taking a Grand Slam . . .
but fell at the final hurdle!

10 April 1954	vs France at Stade Colombes in Paris (lost 3–11)
17 March 1990	vs Scotland at Murrayfield (lost 7–13)*
11 April 1999	vs Wales at Wembley Stadium (lost 31–32)
2 April 2000	vs Scotland at Murrayfield (lost 13–19)
20 October 2001	vs Ireland at Lansdowne Road (lost 14–20)

* Grand Slam decider between teams with 100% records before
the match.

— OVAL BALL AND ROUND BALL —

Just three players have won caps for England at both rugby union and
association football:

Reginald Birkett, who has the honour of scoring England's first ever
try in the inaugural rugby test match in 1871, also played in goal
for England against Scotland at Kennington Oval on 5 April 1879.
He conceded four goals but England won 5–4. Birkett later made
two England rugby appearances at the Oval against Scotland and
Ireland in 1876 and 1877, and also played in the FA Cup final in
1879 and 1880 for Clapham Rovers, who were founder members of
the RFU!

Charles Wilson was capped twice for England at football in 1884,
three years after his one rugby appearance for England against Wales
at Blackheath in 1881. An all-round sportsman, he also gained blues
at Cambridge University for cricket and cycling.

John Sutcliffe, played for England against the New Zealand Natives
at Blackheath in February 1889, scoring a try and a conversion in his
only rugby test appearance. Another goalkeeper, Sutcliffe played in
the 1894 FA Cup final for Bolton and gained five soccer caps for
England between 1893 and 1903.

— DRAWING A BLANK —

Eleven England matches have ended 0–0 at full-time. They are:

Date	Result	Venue
3 Mar 1873	Scotland 0, England 0	Glasgow
8 Mar 1875	Scotland 0, England 0	Edinburgh
4 Mar 1878	England 0, Scotland 0	Kennington Oval
13 Mar 1886*	Scotland 0, England 0	Edinburgh
8 Jan 1887*	Wales 0, England 0	Llanelli
10 Mar 1900	Scotland 0, England 0	Inverleith
12 Feb 1910	England 0, Ireland 0	Twickenham
15 Mar 1930	England 0, Scotland 0	Twickenham
18 Jan 1936	Wales 0, England 0	Swansea
20 Jan 1962	England 0, Wales 0	Twickenham
9 Feb 1963	Ireland 0, England 0	Dublin

* successive matches

In addition, since the introduction of points scoring in 1889, England have failed to score in a further 35 matches which they have lost.

— THREE FROM CARDIFF PLAY FOR ENGLAND —

On only two occasions have three players born in the same town played together in an England team, on 11 February 1922 against Ireland at Lansdowne Road and on 25 February 1922 against France at Twickenham. In the England pack for those games were Geoffrey Conway, Ernest Gardner and Robert Duncan – curiously, all three were not even born in England but in Cardiff!

— TRAGEDY STRIKES YOUNG —

Richard Calvert Stafford, a promising prop from Bedford Modern School, made his England debut against Wales at Twickenham in January 1912 at the tender age of 18 and also played against Ireland, Scotland and France in that season's Five Nations Championship. Shortly afterwards, however, Stafford was diagnosed with spinal cancer, and he died at home in Bedford two months before his 20th birthday. He is the youngest test player in world rugby to die.

— ODD JOB —

In the days before professionalism a number of England internationals had unusual occupations:

Carl Aarvold	High Court Judge
Lancelot Barrington-Ward	Surgeon to King George VI 1936–52
Barrie Bennetts	County Coroner
Reginald Birkett	Hide and skin broker
Matthew Bradby	Tea grower
Harry Bradshaw	Horse teamster
William Bromet	Director of the Royal Mint
Carson Catcheside	Coal importer
Bevan Chantrill	Gold miner in South Africa
Leonard Corbett	General manager of a chocolate factory
John Daniell	Tea planter
Maffer Davey	Gold miner in South Africa
Wallace Eyres	Manager of White City Stadium
Stephen Finney	Railway Manager in India
Edward Fraser	Councillor of Government of Mauritius
Harry Garnett	Paper manufacturer
Lyndhurst Giblin	Gold miner in the Klondike
Jenny Greenwood	Company director Boots the Chemists
Anthony Henniker-Gotley	Political officer in Tanganyika
Thomas Holgarth	Shipyard blacksmith
Francis Isherwood	Oil prospector
Joe Kendrew	Governor of Western Australia
William Milton	Private secretary to Cecil Rhodes 1890–96
William Mitchell	Gold miner in South Africa
Philip Moore	Private secretary to HM Queen Elizabeth II 1966–72
Charles Newbold	Managing director Guinness
William Oldham	Workhouse master
Cherry Pillman	Flour importer at the London Corn Exchange
James Pitman	Director at the Bank of England 1941–45
John Rhodes	Glassblower
Geoffrey Roberts	Prosecutor at the Nuremberg War Trials
Courteney Verelst	Coffee planter in Ceylon
Roger Wilson	Professor of surgery Indian Army
Frank Wright	Manager of tea and rubber estates Ceylon

— 17 FOR PELOUS —

French lock Fabien Pelous has played more games against England than any other player, 17 (15 starts and two replacements). The world's record cap holder, Wallaby George Gregan, has played in 16 (15 starts, one replacement), whilst Ireland's Mike Gibson and Philippe Sella both appeared in 15 tests (all starts) against England. Gibson in fact played in every minute of his 15 games.

In addition to these four players, two others have spent more than 1,000 minutes of playing time against England: legendary Irish second-row Willie-John McBride and Welsh wing Gareth Thomas.

— THE TRAGEDY OF FLIGHT 981 —

The day after the France–England match at the new Parc des Princes stadium in Paris on 2 March 1974 news filtered through of the crash of a Turkish Airlines DC10 in a forest close to the town of Senlis in northern France en route from Orly airport to Heathrow.

Ordinarily there would have been little English connection with such a flight, but many passengers who had been stranded at Orly due to a strike by British European Airways employees had transferred over to the ill fated flight. At first it was feared that the England rugby team was on board, but it later emerged that 18 members of the Bury St Edmunds team who were in Paris for the international had perished along with all 327 other people aboard in what was the worst crash in aviation history up to this date.

— EXPERIENCE IN RESERVE —

England's most experienced bench ever had a staggering combined caps total of 319 amongst the seven players named. Amazingly, this record has occurred twice.

Versus Italy in Rome in the Six Nations Championship on 7 April 2002; Martin Johnson (96), Jason Leonard (47), Lawrence Dallaglio (43), Matt Dawson (46), Austin Healey (15), Dorian West (3) and Charlie Hodgson (0).

Versus Ireland at Twickenham on 18 March 2006; Steve Thompson (46), Perry Freshwater (2), Danny Grewcock (63), Lawrence Dallaglio (77), Matt Dawson (76), Dave Walder (4) and Mike Tindall (48).

— FREQUENT SKIPPERS —

A list of the players who have appeared in the most matches as captain of the England rugby team, with England's record under their stewardship. The 'Not Captain' column signifies how many England games they started with someone else as captain on the day.

Games	Name	Period	Record	Not Captain
59	Will Carling	1988–1996	W44, D1, L14	13
39	Martin Johnson	1998–2003	W34, L5	43
22	Lawrence Dallaglio	1997–2004	W10, D2, L10	63
21	Bill Beaumont	1978–1982	W11, D2, L8	12
17	Martin Corry	2005–2007	W9, L8	47
15	Phil Vickery	2002–2007	W10, L5	49

— 'HEATH, ACE OF CLUBS —

One hundred and eighty four different clubs have supplied England players but Blackheath are the only team to have had over 100 players capped for England whilst playing their rugby for the club. They are head and shoulders above second placed Harlequins with 33 more players capped for their country.

Below is a list of all the teams who have produced over 20 players who have been capped from clubs whilst they have been playing their rugby at the named club:

Club	Players
Blackheath	122
Harlequins	90
Oxford University	81
Cambridge University	79
Leicester	74
Richmond	64
Gloucester	62
Wasps	54
Bath	52
Bristol	50
Northampton	46
Coventry	41
Sale	31
Liverpool	26
Manchester	25
Moseley	24

Bedford	21
Headingley	21
Saracens	21
Royal Navy	20

In terms of individual caps won whilst at clubs, Leicester players have earned 1,097 caps, followed by Harlequins with 790. Those Tigers players have amassed 163 tries and 1,137 points for England, which are also both records.

— SHORT CHANGED —

When the New Zealand Natives (the former name given to the New Zealand Maori) visited these shores for their tour in 1889 they faced England at the Rectory Field in Blackheath on 16 February.

During the match, English three-quarter Drewy Stoddart lost his shorts during a tackle by the Natives' forward Thomas Ellison. Stoddart immediately stopped, threw down the ball, and most of the Maori players formed the customary cordon around him while he changed.

Whilst this was happening England and Burton forward Frank Evershed picked up the ball and walked over for an unopposed try. The English referee Mr Rowland Hill, who was Honorary Secretary of the RFU at the time, awarded the score but The Natives vigorously disputed it and George Williams, Richard Taiaroa and Sherry Wynyard walked from the field in disgust.

Several minutes elapsed before James Scott, the manager of the Natives team, persuaded his men to retake the field and finish the match, which Mr Hill had restarted without them.

— PURPLE PATCHES —

Flying winger Rory Underwood, of the RAF and Leicester, holds the record for scoring at least one try in successive England matches, with a total of nine tries in six consecutive games in 1988. He began his impressive run with a pair of tries against Ireland at Twickenham in the Five Nations Championship on 19 March 1988. Underwood then touched down against Ireland in Dublin (Millennium Trophy); in both tests away to Australia; notched a brace against Fiji in Suva; and, finally, grabbing another pair against the Wallabies at Twickenham on 5 November 1998.

Only two other players have scored tries in five successive England games: Tot Robinson doing so in his first five appearances between

1897–1900. Robinson's England career lasted for a total of just eight matches and he scored tries in seven of them, just missing out in the nil-nil draw with Scotland at Inverleith on 10 March 1900.

Will Greenwood also scored tries in five consecutive games. His purple patch began on 2 December 2000 against the Springboks at Twickenham and ended when he failed to score in the Grand Slam match against Ireland in Dublin in October 2001.

— SUCCESSFUL SCHOOLS —

Appropriately enough, Rugby School has provided England with more internationals than any other school or college:

No players	School
47	Rugby School
33	Marlborough College
30	Cheltenham College
27	Bedford School
24	Clifton College
24	Uppingham School
22	Tonbridge School

Rugby at Rugby

— THE FINISHERS —

The England players who have averaged better than a try every 80 minutes:

Name	Tries	Caps	Mins	Mins/try
Hugh Vyvyan	1	0+1	13	13.00
Howard Marshall	3	1	80	26.67
Martyn Wood	1	0+2	46	46.00
Graham Meikle	4	3	240	60.00
Vincent Coates	6	5	400	66.67
Henry Taylor	6	5	400	66.67
Daniel Lambert	8	7	560	70.00
Arthur Hudson	9	8	640	71.11

— SUCCESSFUL NEW BOYS —

Daniel Lambert, a 23-year-old winger with Harlequins, holds the record for the most tries on an England debut with five against France at the Athletic Ground in Richmond on 5 January 1907.

Four other players have scored debut hat-tricks for England: forward Harry Vassall against Wales at Blackheath in 1881; three-quarter Gregory Wade against Wales at Swansea a year later; half-back Howard Marshall, also against Wales at Cardiff in 1893; and, finally, Jeremy Guscott versus Romania in Bucharest on 13 May 1989.

Intriguingly, George Wade only played because first-choice winger Philip Newton got lost on the way to Swansea!

Charlie Hodgson's 44 points on debut against Romania on 17 November 2001 is also the most points scored by any individual in an England shirt. Hodgson scored two tries, 14 conversions and two penalty goals, landing 16 out of 22 kicks at goal.

Just two front rowers have scored a try on England debut: Derek Teden against Wales at Twickenham on 21 January 1939 and Mark Linnett against Fiji at Twickenham on 4 November 1989.

Only five England players have begun their international careers with tries in each of their first three appearances: Tot Robinson (1897), Carston Catcheside (1924), Graham Meikle (1934), Jeremy Guscott (1989) and Mark Cueto (2004). Of these players, Robinson, Catcheside and Guscott also added tries on their fourth appearances, while Robinson uniquely went on to score a try on the occasion of his fifth cap.

— QUICKEST CENTURY —

The least number of games played by an England player before passing 100 international points:

Name	Cap	Opponent (Venue)	Date
Paul Grayson	6th	v Scotland (Twickenham)	1 Feb 1997
Simon Hodgkinson	8th	v Argentina (Buenos Aires)	4 Aug 1990
Jonny Wilkinson	10th	v Canada (Twickenham)	28 Aug 1999
Dusty Hare	13th	v France (Paris)	20 Feb 1982
Jon Webb	13th	v Scotland (Twickenham)	4 Feb 1989
Bob Hiller	14th	v France (Twickenham)	27 Feb 1971
Charlie Hodgson	14th	v Australia (Twickenham)	27 Nov 2004

Fastest 200 Career Points

Simon Hodgkinson	14th	v United States (Twickenham)	11 Oct 1991
Paul Grayson	15th	v Ireland (Twickenham)	4 Apr 1998
Jonny Wilkinson	16th	v France (Paris)	19 Feb 2000
Dusty Hare	22nd	v France (Paris)	3 Mar 1984

Fastest 300 Career Points

Jonny Wilkinson	22nd	v Argentina (Twickenham)	25 Nov 2000
Paul Grayson	23rd	v South Africa (Paris)	24 Oct 1999

Fastest 400 Career Points

Jonny Wilkinson	27th	v France (Twickenham)	7 Apr 2001
Paul Grayson	32nd	v Ireland (Twickenham)	6 Mar 2004

— ON THE BIG SCREEN —

Video referees or television match officials (TMOs) were first called upon to make decisions on the validity of a try being scored in 2000. The first occasion involving England of a score being referred to the TMO was on 17 June 2000 at Loftus Versfeld in Pretoria when South African official Mark Lawrence adjudged that England's Tim Stimpson did not appear to have the ball in his hands and so was denied a penalty try.

— TRY HAT-TRICKS —

A total of 32 hat-tricks by 25 different players have been scored for England.

Jason Robinson and Jeremy Guscott lead the way, with three hat-tricks each, while Cyril Lowe, Rory Underwood and Chris Oti all accomplished the feat twice. Just three forwards have scored three tries in the same game: Neil Back vs Netherlands at Huddersfield in 1998, and George Burton and Henry Vassall both vs Wales at Blackheath in 1881.

A dozen different players have bagged three tries in a test against England: Michel Crauste (France), Danie Gerber (South Africa), Jehoida Hodges (Wales), Steve Larkham (Australia), Willie Llewellyn (Wales), Jonah Lomu (New Zealand), Duncan McGregor (New Zealand), Clyde Rathbone (South Africa), Maurice Richards (Wales), Joe Rokocoko (New Zealand), Ben Tune (Australia) and Bryan Williams (New Zealand). The only forwards among this list are Crauste, for France at Paris in 1962, and Hodges, who scored a hat-trick for Wales at Swansea in 1903.

The most tries scored by an England player without the aid of a hat-trick is 16, by Matt Dawson and Lawrence Dallaglio. Both, coincidentally, played in 77 test match appearances apiece. Richard Hill holds the record for the most tries (11) without scoring more than one in a single game.

— FAMILIAR REFS —

The referee who has taken charge of most England matches is Mr Albert Freethy, a Welsh whistler who took charge of 15 England games between 1923 and 1931. Scotsman Jim Fleming is in second place with 12 games between 1985 and 2000, including the England-France fixture he refereed at Twickenham in 1999 after taking over from injured New Zealander Colin Hawke.

Two other Welshmen have officiated at 11 England matches: T.D. Schofield (1907–21) and Gwynne Walters (1959–66).

Tommy Vile of Wales was England's good luck charm between 1923 and 1928, refereeing eight games in which England remained unbeaten. On the other side of the coin, Scotsman Norman Sanson took charge of four matches that England failed to win between 1978 and 1979.

— ENGLAND LEGENDS: RORY UNDERWOOD —

Rory Underwood was born to be a wing. Blessed not only with natural speed but also great strength, he become England's top international try scorer with 49 touchdowns.

Much of Underwood's childhood was spent in Malaysia, before he attended Barnard Castle School in Durham where he discovered rugby and also shone at cricket and swimming.

The brother of fellow England star Tony, Underwood made his international debut against Ireland in 1984 and scored the first of his England tries in the following game against France. During England's home game with Fiji in 1989 he scored five tries, equalling the individual record set by Douglas Lambert 82 years earlier against France.

Underwood contributed to the England Grand Slams of 1991, 1992, and 1995; in fact, the flying winger played some part in every Five Nations championship between 1984 and 1996. Incredibly, he played in every minute of the last 10 of these campaigns, a total of 42 games in a row.

Rory featured in the inaugural World Cup in Australasia in 1987 and was in the England team which reached the 1991 World Cup final at Twickenham. He became the first England player to reach fifty caps

*Flt Lieutenant Rory
Underwood takes off*

during that tournament with his appearance in the semi-final against Scotland. He also travelled to South Africa for the 1995 competition, scoring five tries to take his World cup total to 11.

A former flight lieutenant in the RAF, Rory is now a partner in a management development consultancy with former Gulf War POW John Peters.

Rory Underwood MBE Factfile
Born: 19 Jun 1963 in Middlesbrough, Yorkshire
Clubs: Middlesbrough, Leicester, Bedford
Caps: 85 (W55, D2, L28)
Scoring: 49 tries – 210 pts
England debut: 18 Feb 1984 vs Ireland (Twickenham)

— SHIRT SPONSORS —

The first time England ever carried a main sponsor's name on their shirts was for the visit of Italy to Twickenham on 23 November 1996. The original sponsor's name, 'Cellnet', was changed slightly to 'Bt Cellnet' on 5 February 2000 for the home match with Ireland in the inaugural Six Nations Championship. 'Bt Cellnet' evolved into 'O$_2$', which appeared on the players' shirts for the first time in Buenos Aires for the match with Argentina on 22 June 2002.

During this time, England were not allowed to carry any shirt sponsorship in any of the Rugby World Cups, including both qualifying games in 1998 and the finals in 1999, 2003 and 2007.

— ENGLAND AT THE FOURTH RUGBY WORLD CUP: 1999 —

Games and Scorers:
Qualifying (1998)
Europe Group 2

14 Nov	Holland	Huddersfield	W 110–0	t: Back 4, Guscott 4, Greenwood, Cockerill, Corry, Dawson, Luger, Healey, Beal, penalty try. c: Grayson 15
22 Nov	Italy	Huddersfield	W 23–15	t: Luger, Greenwood. c: Grayson 2. p: Grayson 3

RWC Europe Group 2 Qualifying Table:

Nation	P	W	D	L	F	A	Pts	Tries
England	2	2	0	0	133	15	6	18
Italy	2	1	0	1	82	30	4	11
Netherlands	2	0	0	2	7	177	2	1

Squad and Appearances:

Coach: Clive Woodward.   Captain: Martin Johnson.

Garath Archer (Newcastle Falcons) NL/It; Neil Back (Leicester Tigers) NL/It; Nick Beal (Northampton Saints) NL(r); Mike Catt (Bath) NL(r)/It(r); Ben Clarke (Richmond) NL/It; Richard Cockerill (Leicester Tigers) NL/It; Martin Corry (Leicester Tigers) NL/It; Matt Dawson (Northampton Saints) NL/It; Phil De Glanville (Bath); Darren Garforth (Leicester Tigers) NL/It; Paul Grayson (Northampton Saints) NL/It; Phil Greening (Sale Sharks); Will Greenwood (Leicester Tigers) NL/It; Danny Grewcock (Saracens); Jerry Guscott (Bath) NL/It; Austin Healey (Leicester Tigers) NL/It; Richard Hill (Saracens) NL(r)/It(r); Martin Johnson (Leicester Tigers) NL/It; Jason Leonard (NEC Harlequins) NL/It; Dan Luger (NEC Harlequins) NL/It; Matt Perry (Bath) NL/It; Tim Rodber (Northampton Saints) NL(r)/It(r); Graham Rowntree (Leicester Tigers) NL(r)/It(r).

Scoring:

Name	T	C	P	D	Pts
Paul Grayson	-	17	3	-	43
Neil Back	4	-	-	-	20
Jerry Guscott	4	-	-	-	20
Will Greenwood	2	-	-	-	10
Dan Luger	2	-	-	-	10
Nick Beal	1	-	-	-	5
Richard Cockerill	1	-	-	-	5
Martin Corry	1	-	-	-	5
Matt Dawson	1	-	-	-	5
Austin Healey	1	-	-	-	5
PENALTY TRY	1	-	-	-	5
TOTALS	18	17	3	0	133
AGAINST	0	0	4	1	15

Finals
Pool B

2 Oct	Italy	Twickenham	W 67–7	t: Dawson, Hill, De Glanville, Perry, Wilkinson, Luger, Back, Corry. c: Wilkinson 6. p: Wilkinson 5
9 Oct	N Zealand	Twickenham	L 16–30	t: De Glanville. c: Wilkinson. p: Wilkinson 3
15 Oct	Tonga	Twickenham	W 101–10	t: Greenwood 2, Healey 2, Greening 2, Luger 2, Guscott 2, Dawson, Perry, Hill. c: Grayson 12. p: Grayson 4

RWC Pool B Table:

Nation	P	W	D	L	F	A	Pts	Tries
New Zealand	3	3	0	0	176	28	9	22
England	3	2	0	1	184	47	7	22
Tonga	3	1	0	2	47	171	5	4
Italy	3	0	0	3	35	196	3	2

Play-off

20 Oct	Fiji	Twickenham	W 45–24	t: Luger, Back, Beal, Greening. c: Wilkinson, Dawson. p: Wilkinson 7

Quarter-final

24 Oct	S Africa	Paris	L 21–44	p: Grayson 6, Wilkinson

Squad and Appearances:
Head coach: Clive Woodward. Coach: Andy Robinson.
Captain: Martin Johnson.
Garath Archer (Newcastle Falcons) T/Fj; Neil Back (Leicester Tigers) It/NZ/Fj/SA; Nick Beal (Northampton Saints) It(r)/T(r)/Fj/SA; Mike Catt (Bath) T(r)/Fj/SA(r); Richard Cockerill (Leicester Tigers) It/NZ/T(r)/Fj(r); Martin Corry (Leicester Tigers) It(r)/NZ(r)/SA(r);

Lawrence Dallaglio (London Wasps) It/NZ/T/Fj/SA; Matt Dawson (Northampton Saints) It/NZ/T/Fj(r)/SA; Phil De Glanville (Bath) It/NZ/Fj(r)/SA; Darren Garforth (Leicester Tigers) It(r)/NZ(r)/Fj; Paul Grayson (Northampton Saints) NZ(r)/T/Fj(r)/SA; Phil Greening (Sale Sharks) It(r)/NZ(r)/T/Fj/SA; Will Greenwood (Leicester Tigers) It/T/Fj/SA; Danny Grewcock (Saracens) It/NZ/T(r)/SA; Jerry Guscott (Bath) It(r)/NZ/T; Austin Healey (Leicester Tigers) It/NZ/T/Fj/SA(r); Richard Hill (Saracens) It/NZ/T/Fj(r)/SA; Martin Johnson (Leicester Tigers) It/NZ/T/Fj/SA; Jason Leonard (NEC Harlequins) It/NZ/Fj/SA; Leon Lloyd (Leicester Tigers); Dan Luger (Saracens) It/NZ/T/Fj/SA; Neil McCarthy (Gloucester); Matt Perry (Bath) It/NZ/T/Fj/SA; Tim Rodber (Northampton Saints) NZ(r)/Fj(r); Graham Rowntree (Leicester Tigers) It(r)/T/Fj(r); Victor Ubogu (Bath); Phil Vickery (Gloucester) It/NZ/T/SA; Jonny Wilkinson (Newcastle Falcons) It/NZ/Fj/SA(r); Martyn Wood (London Wasps); Joe Worsley (London Wasps) T/Fj.
Appearances as a replacement marked with (r).

Scoring:

Name	T	C	P	D	Pts
Jonny Wilkinson	1	8	16	-	69
Paul Grayson	-	12	10	-	54
Dan Luger	4	-	-	-	20
Phil Greening	3	-	-	-	15
Matt Dawson	2	1	-	-	12
Neil Back	2	-	-	-	10
Phil De Glanville	2	-	-	-	10
Will Greenwood	2	-	-	-	10
Jerry Guscott	2	-	-	-	10
Austin Healey	2	-	-	-	10
Richard Hill	2	-	-	-	10
Matt Perry	2	-	-	-	10
Nick Beal	1	-	-	-	5
Martin Corry	1	-	-	-	5
TOTALS	26	21	26	0	250
AGAINST	10	10	10	5	115

— EXPERIENCE IS THE KEY —

The most experienced England team of all time was the one which played against Wales in the quarter-final of the 2003 Rugby World Cup at Brisbane's Suncorp Stadium. The 15 England players had amassed the staggering total of 689 caps, and lined up as follows: Jason Robinson (25 caps), Dan Luger (37), Will Greenwood (44), Mike Tindall (30), Ben Cohen (32), Jonny Wilkinson (49), Matt Dawson (54), Jason Leonard (110), Steve Thompson (21), Phil Vickery (35), Martin Johnson (81), Ben Kay (25), Lewis Moody (21), Lawrence Dallaglio (62), Neil Back (63).

The least experienced England team is, predictably, the one which took to the field for the first post-war international match in 1947, after six years of hostilities and eight years after the last official England rugby match. Just one of England's XV on duty that day had played before the war – Waterloo wing Dickie Guest, who had gained three caps in the final three games of 1939.

— A SWARM OF BACK-ROW WASPS —

When James Haskell, Tom Rees and Joe Worsley were named in the England starting lineup for the Six Nations match against Wales at the Millennium Stadium on 17 March 2007, it marked the first occasion that England's entire starting back row all came from the same club – in this instance London Wasps. As it was, the partnership lasted just nine minutes before Worsley retired injured to be replaced by Sale's Magnus Lund.

— JUST TWO THOUSAND —

The smallest attendance for an England game was 2,000 for the visit of Wales to Cardigan Fields, Leeds on 5 January 1884. It was the only international ever played at the venue and was England's first match in Yorkshire. England, captained by Temple Gurdon, rewarded the hardy souls who bothered to turn out by winning by one goal and two tries to a goal.

— ROSE'S ROUND —

When England arrived in Cardiff in 1987 they hadn't won in the Welsh capital for 24 years. The two sets of forwards were at each other's throats from the outset, Wade Dooley breaking the cheekbone of Phil Davies with a wild haymaker tackle. After the match Dooley, Gareth Chilcott, Graham Dawe and captain Richard Hill all picked up suspensions for their various on-field indiscretions.

The Welsh crowd were so incensed by the English antics that they begun to hurl coins at visiting full back Marcus Rose. Completely unfazed, Rose picked up the loose change from the turf and handed the princely sum of £3.50 to Scottish referee Ray Megson for safekeeping. After the match, which England lost yet again, Rose retrieved the money and spent it in the bar!

— GOING 'HOME' TO PLAY —

A number of non-English born players have represented England in the country of their birth.

Mike Catt, Nick Abendanon and Matt Stevens are the only South African-born England players to appear for their adopted country in the Republic. Catt doing so on eight occasions between 1995 and 2000, including six matches during the 1995 Rugby World Cup competition.

Kyran Bracken is the only Dublin-born Englishman to have played for England at Lansdowne Road, featuring in four matches between 1995 and 2003. Wilfred Bolton, who was born in Ireland, turned out on three occasions for England at Lansdowne Road between 1882 and1887.

Cardiff-born players Ernest Gardner and Geoffrey Conway played for England at the Arms Park in 1922. Another eleven Wales-born players have played for England in the Principality: Arthur Evanson, John Mathias, John Kendall-Carpenter, Reg Edwards, William Hancock, Peter Woodruff, George Thomas, William Morgan, Simon Halliday, Dewi Morris and Dorian West.

John Eddison, who was born in Edinburgh, played for England at Inverleith in 1912. Additionally, Benjamin Burns, Alastair Smallwood, Roderick MacLennan, Alan Henderson were all born in Scotland and have appeared for England in the land of kilts and haggis.

— PHANTOM FOG —

On 18 January 1908 England played their only ever match at Ashton Gate, Bristol, the visit of Wales attracting a good crowd of 25,000. Wales won a nine-try thriller 28–18 but, because of a thick fog which enveloped the ground, the spectators only caught glimpses of the action. Newspaper reports spoke of, "phantom figures flitting to and fro in the thick fog that shrouded the ground."

— ENGLAND LEGENDS: WADE DOOLEY —

A six-foot, eight-inch police constable known as the 'Blackpool Tower', Wade Dooley was a formidable force in the lineout and scrum for England during a 55-cap international career spanning nine seasons.

Dooley was a rugby league player in his early days before switching over to union aged 18 to play for Preston Grasshoppers. Ten years later, he was plucked from relative obscurity to answer England's call after just 20 minutes of representative rugby experience, for the North against Romania in December 1984. Despite his late arrival on the international scene, Dooley eventually became his country's most capped lock, until surpassed by Martin Johnson.

A stalwart in the pack during two World Cups, he formed a durable partnership in the England boiler room with Paul Ackford, the pair helping their country reach the final of the 1991 event.

Wade Anthony Dooley Factfile
Born: 2 Oct 1957 in Warrington, Cheshire
Clubs: Preston Grasshoppers, Fylde
Caps: 55 (W33, D2, L20)
Scoring: 3 tries – 12 pts
England debut: 5 Jan 1985 vs Romania (Twickenham)

— BEATS THE GYM —

John Henry Clayton, a 22-year-old former Rugby schoolboy who made his only international appearance in the very first test match in 1871, had an unusual fitness regime for the match, as this record reveals. "For a month prior to the match he ran four miles every morning in the dark before breakfast, with a large Newfoundland dog to make the pace. After a four-mile horseback ride to his office, he worked 8am to 8pm before taking a four-mile ride home to a dinner of underdone beef with beer!"

— COCKERILL TAKES ON THE HAKA —

On 22 November 1997, England lined up to face New Zealand at Old Trafford, Manchester United's legendary 'theatre of dreams'. Just before kick-off the All Blacks stood in a semi-circle around their own 10 metre line to began their famous pre-match ritual, the haka.

Rather than simply waiting for the show to end like the rest of his team-mates, England hooker Richard Cockerill picked out his opposite number, Norm Hewitt, and began to advance just over the half-way line. Hewitt responded by moving forward, so that by the time the New Zealanders had finished their war-like chant the pair were eyeball to eyeball.

"I believe that I did the right thing," Cockerill later told reporters. "They were throwing down a challenge and I showed them I was ready to accept it." Despite Cockerill's show of bravado, the All Blacks still won the match fairly comfortably.

— DROP KINGS —

The full list of players who have scored more than one drop goal for England:

Player		Career	Drops	Caps
1	Jonny Wilkinson	1998–2008	29	66+4
2	Rob Andrew	1985–1997	21	69+2
3	Paul Grayson	1995–2004	6	24+8
4=	Les Cusworth	1979–1988	4	12
4=	John Horton	1978–1984	4	13
6=	John Finlan	1967–1973	3	13
6=	Richard Sharp	1960–1967	3	14
6=	Alan Old	1972–1978	3	16
6=	Nim Hall	1947–1955	3	17
6=	Dave Davies	1913–1923	3	22
6=	Charlie Hodgson	2001–2008	3	25+5
6=	Mike Catt	1994–2007	3	62+13
13=	Harold Freeman	1872–1874	2	3
13=	Dick Cowman	1971–1973	2	5
13=	Lennard Stokes	1875–1881	2	12
13=	Fred Byrne	1894–1899	2	13
13=	Peter Cranmer	1934–1938	2	16
13=	Bob Hiller	1968–1972	2	19
13=	Jerry Guscott	1989–1999	2	62+3

— ENGLAND LEGENDS:
PETER WINTERBOTTOM —

A one time farmer, Yorkshireman Peter Winterbottom was the scourge of opposing fly halves for over a decade. For much of the 1980s, no England international was complete without the sight of Winterbottom's trademark flowing blonde locks trailing behind him as he relentlessly chased down the number 10 from his position of openside flanker.

One of the best number 7s world rugby has ever seen, Winterbottom gained 58 caps between 1982 and 1993. He played in the 1991 Rugby World Cup final at Twickenham, as well as being part of two Grand Slam squads in 1991 and 1992. He retired from the international game as England's most capped flanker.

Much travelled, Winterbottom appeared in the National Provincial Championship in New Zealand and the Currie Cup in South Africa, as well as playing for Headingley and Harlequins in England, skippering the latter to three successive Pilkington Cup finals.

Peter James Winterbottom Factfile
Born: 31 May 1960 in Horsforth, Leeds
Clubs: Fleetwood, Headingley, Exeter, Napier HS OB (NZ), Hawke's Bay (NZ), Durban HS OB (South Africa), Transvaal (South Africa), Meralomas (Canada), Harlequins
Caps: 58 (W31, D2, L25)
Scoring: 3 tries – 13 pts
England debut: 2 Jan 1982 vs Australia (Twickenham)

— A JOB LOT OF JOHNS —

The most popular forenames of England internationals (these names are not necessarily the ones that players were known by and, additionally, include all middle names):

John	186
William	119
James	82
Henry	69
Edward	65
Charles	64
Robert	57
Thomas	57
George	54
Arthur	52

— DALLAGLIO'S 28 WINS —

Lawrence Dallaglio achieved a remarkable run of success when he was on the winning team in 28 successive England matches. The sequence began with victory over South Africa at Bloemfontein on 24 June 2000, and did not end until England lost to Ireland at Twickenham in 2004.

— SNOW JOKE —

When Scotland made the trip south to play England in March 1947 it was in the midst of one of the worst winters on record. Hardly any players had played rugby since mid January and the game took place on a near frozen pitch, hence many were injured and in the days before replacements both sides were on occasion down to 13 men.

Just getting to the match was a challenge. The Scotland team endured a 20 hour journey on the Thursday before the game whilst Duncan McKean, who travelled later, did not join his team mates until 6am on the morning of the match having spent all day and night on a train which had neither a restaurant car nor sleeping carriage.

England forward Micky Steele-Bodger was just as unfortunate. He was a student at the Royal Dick Veterinary College in Edinburgh and his own train had to be dug out of the snow twice before reaching Carlisle and he too only arrived in London in the early hours of Saturday morning.

— NO ANTHEM —

Shortly before the start of the match between England and New Zealand at Twickenham on 4 January 1964 the teams were recalled to the dressing room after their warm up. The band also left the pitch and failed to reappear for the playing of the national anthems. This is the only occasion in modern times that the national anthem has not been played at Twickenham prior to an international match.

— MAKE MINE A TRIPLE —

The origins of the name 'triple crown' are not known. The first recorded use of the term appears in *The Irish Times*'s match report of the encounter between Ireland and Wales on 12 March 1894: "After long years of seemingly hopeless struggle Ireland has achieved the triple crown honours of Rugby football," the newspaper reported.

The name may derive from the Triple Crown of James I/VI who was the first King to rule over England, Scotland and Ireland – Wales, at that time, being considered as part of England and not a separate country. This theory is backed up by a reference in Shakespeare's masterpiece *Macbeth*: in Act 4, Scene I, Macbeth refers to King James's "treble sceptre".

As no trophy was historically awarded for winning the Triple Crown, it was often called 'the invisible cup'. There have been attempts, however, to create a trophy for the competition. In 1975, for instance, a retired miner by the name of Dave Marrington got to work with his penknife and turned a lump of coal hewn from the Haig Colliery in Cumbria into a surprisingly ornate work. Marrington's creation features a crown sitting on a four-sided base on which are represented a rose, a shamrock, a thistle and the Prince of Wales feathers. Despite a campaign to have the homemade trophy awarded to the triple crown winners, it was rejected by all four Home unions. It is kept today in the Museum of Rugby at Twickenham.

Eventually, in 2006, the primary sponsor of the competition, the Royal Bank of Scotland, commissioned a trophy to be awarded to the Triple Crown winners. The silver dish known as the Triple Crown trophy, was contested for the first time in the 2006 Six Nations. Ireland were the inaugural winners, captain Brian O'Driscoll recieving the trophy at Twickenham on March 18.

England have claimed the triple crown on 23 occasions including four in succession between 1995 and 1998.

— 198 WITH A TIGER —

When England took on South Africa in Bloemfontein on 26 May 2007 they did so without a current member from Leicester Tigers in their ranks. This was the first time that no Tigers were selected since England visited Scotland at Murrayfield on 15 February 1986, some 198 test matches before.

— MIXING SPORT WITH POLITICS —

England internationals who doubled up as members of Parliament:

Walter Elliot	Tory MP for Carshalton & Banstead 1960–70
Alfred Hamersley	Tory MP for Woodstock 1910–18
Arthur Heath	Tory MP for Henley 1900 and Leek in 1910
James Pitman	Tory MP for Bath 1945–64
Percy Royds	Tory MP for Kingston-upon-Thames 1937–45
Wavell Wakefield	Tory MP for Swindon 1935 and Marylebone 1945–63
Derek Wyatt	Labour MP for Sittingbourne & Sheppey 1997–

— COOK CUP —

The Cook Cup was established in 1997 when Australia and England contracted to play each other bi-annually for the next 10 years, on a home and away basis. The cup is named after Captain James Cook (1728–1779), the noted English explorer, navigator and cartographer who claimed the east coast of Australia as a British discovery. Made from crystal glass, the cup was designed by Royal Doulton in London.

The longest tenure is by England who held the trophy for almost four years between 2000 and 2004.

— NOTHING TO SEPARATE —

England drew 38 of their first 310 matches up until 1971, but they have drawn just 10 more in their next 270 encounters to date. Here's a list of those recent tied matches:

Date	Result	Venue
27 Feb 1971	England 14, France 14	Twickenham
2 Mar 1974	France 12, England 12	Paris
3 Feb 1979	England 7, Scotland 7	Twickenham
30 May 1981	Argentina 19, England 19	Buenos Aires
16 Jan 1982	Scotland 9, England 9	Murrayfield
5 Feb 1983	Wales 13, England 13	Cardiff
2 Feb 1985	England 9, France 9	Twickenham
4 Feb 1989	England 12, Scotland 12	Twickenham
15 Nov 1997	England 15, Australia 15	Twickenham
6 Dec 1997	England 26, New Zealand 26	Twickenham

— POACHERS TURNED GAMEKEEPERS —

Of the England players who later took up the whistle, Vincent Cartwright is unique in refereeing a test match *before* he won his last cap. Cartwright had a busy 1906 skippering England in their first two matches of that season's Four Nations Championship against Wales and Ireland, before donning his referee's uniform for the Ireland-Scotland game at Lansdowne Road. He then returned to playing duties, captaining England against Scotland on 17 March. Cartwright made two further test appearances as England captain in 1906 before becoming a full-time referee. After taking charge of four further tests, he hung up his whistle in 1911.

	Player		Referee		
Name	Caps	Career	Tests	Career
Arthur Guillemard	2	1871–1872	6	1877–1881
Frederick Currey	1	1872	1	1887
Temple Gurdon	16	1878–1886	2	1898–1899
Frederick Alderson	6	1891–1893	1	1903
Vincent Cartwright	14	1903–1906	5	1906–1911
Bim Baxter	3	1900	9	1913–1925
Jack Miles	1	1903	3	1913–1914
Percy Royds	3	1898–1899	2	1921–1923
Harold Harrison	4	1909–1914	1	1922
Joseph Brunton	3	1914	1	1924
Barry Cumberlege	8	1920–1922	16	1926–1934
Harold Day	4	1920–1926	1	1934
Henry Fry	3	1934	1	1945

— PENALTY TRIES —

Up until the start of the 2007 autumn internationals, England have been awarded a dozen penalty tries and conceded just one. The first was awarded early on in freezing conditions on a snow covered pitch when an Irish boot hacked the ball away from Dean Richards' feet in a scrummage just as the Leicester number eight was about to swoop for the first try on his England debut. Richards needn't have worried, however, by the end of the game he had helped himself to two pushover tries as the English juggernaut pack tore the Irishmen asunder.

The only penalty try England have ever conceded came two weeks later at the Parc des Princes in Paris awarded after England's replacement full-back, Stuart Barnes, deliberately knocked the ball on just as Philippe Sella had given what seemed like a scoring pass to centre partner Denis Charvet.

For England:

Opponent (Venue)	Date	Result	Referee
Ireland (Twickenham)	1 March 1986	Won 25–20	Clive Norling
France (Paris)	15 Feb 1992	Won 31–13	Stephen Hilditch
Romania (Twickenham)	12 Nov 1994	Won 54–3	Stef Neethling
Samoa (Durban)	4 Jun 1995	Won 44–22	Patrick Robin
Scotland (Twickenham)	1 Feb 1997	Won 41–13	Paddy O'Brien
Scotland (Murrayfield)	22 Mar 1998	Won 34–20	Clayton Thomas
Netherlands (Huddersfield)	14 Nov 1998	Won 110–0	Roger Duhau
United States (Twickenham)	21 Aug 1999	Won 106–8	Paul Honiss
Italy (Rome)	18 Mar 2000	Won 59–12	Alan Lewis
Canada (Burnaby)	9 Jun 2001	Won 59–20	Joel Jutge
South Africa (Twickenham)	23 Nov 2002	Won 53–3	Paddy O'Brien
Samoa (Melbourne)	26 Oct 2003	Won 35–22	Jonathan Kaplan

Against:	Date	Result	Referee
For France (Paris)	15 Mar 1986	Lost 10–29	Derek Bevan

— ALWAYS THE LEADER —

Of England's 122 captains only Frederic Stokes skippered the side in all of his internationals. The Blackheath forward led England in his country's first three games, recording a win, a draw and a defeat.

— 95 FOR 3 —

No England international has yet lived to 100, but three did make it to the ripe old age of 95. John Clifford Gibbs, a winger with Harlequins, gained seven caps for England between 1925 and 27 and died in Thanet just two months shy of his 96th birthday in January 1998. Another 'Quin, full-back John Hubbard, made his only test appearance against Scotland at Twickenham in 1930 in a 0–0 draw, and survived until August

1997. Finally, Sale's speedy winger Hal Sever, who won ten caps (1936–38), died in June 2005 also aged 95.

— SIXTY NINE FROM SALE —

When Romania visited Twickenham on 17 November 2001 they suffered the heaviest defeat ever meted out by England (134–0). Sale players contributed no fewer than 69 points towards the England total, easily the highest tally from a single club in one match. Fly-half Charlie Hodgson scored a record 44 points on his own, while full-back Jason Robinson grabbed four tries, and just for good measure replacement flanker Alex Sanderson also added a try!

The most tries by players from a single club is eight by the Leicester Tigers (Neil Back (4 tries), Austin Healey, Will Greenwood, Richard Cockerill and Martin Corry) in the 101–0 win against Netherlands at Huddersfield on 14 November 1998.

— MILLENNIUM TROPHY —

Established in 1988 as part of the city of Dublin's millennial celebrations, the Millennium Trophy was created for a special Ireland-England match but has since been presented to the annual winners of the match between the two countries. The original match, dubbed Dublin Millennium Challenge, was played on 23 April, the only occasion that England have played a game on St George's Day. England won the game 21–10 and were presented with a trophy in the shape of a horned 'Viking' helmet, donated by sponsor Digital.

— NON-ENGLISH CLUBS —

Twenty-six players have been capped by England while playing their club rugby outside the country:

Playing in France
Maurice Colclough (Angouleme, 16 caps, 1978–82)
Rob Andrew (Toulouse, 5 caps, 1992)
Richard Pool-Jones (Stade Français, 1 cap, 1998)
Dan Luger (Perpignan, 5 caps, 2003)
Perry Freshwater (Perpignan, 10 caps, 2005–08)

Playing in Ireland
Peter Young (Wanderers, 9 caps including
2 as captain, 1954–55)

Playing in Scotland
Edward Barrett (Lennox, 1 cap, 1903)
Lancelot Ward (Edinburgh University, 4 caps, 1910)
James Morgan (Hawick, 1 cap, 1920)
Micky Steele-Bodger (Edinburgh University, 5 caps, 1948)
Alan Henderson (Edinburgh Wanderers, 4 caps, 1948–49)
Vic Leadbetter (Edinburgh Wanderers, 2 caps, 1954)
Lionel Weston (West of Scotland, 2 caps, 1972)

Playing in Wales
Samuel Williams (Newport, 4 caps, 1911)
Robert Dibble (Newport, 3 caps all as captain, 1912)
Ernest Hammett (Newport, 7 caps, 1920–21)
Reg Edwards (Newport, 11 caps, 1921–25)
Tom Woods (Pontypool, 1 cap, 1921)
William Hancock (Newport, 2 caps, 1955)
Barry Nelmes (Cardiff, 6 caps, 1975–78)
Mark Keyworth (Swansea, 4 caps, 1976)
John Scott (Cardiff, 30 caps including 4 as captain, 1978–84)
Colin Smart (Newport, 17 caps, 1979–83)
Tony Swift (Swansea, 6 caps, 1981–84)
Maurice Colclough (Swansea, 4 caps, 1986)

Leadbetter, Williams, Hammett and Hancock all made their England debuts in the country where they were playing their club rugby at the time, while the England team for the trip to Cardiff to play Wales on 5 February 1983 included three players playing their club rugby in Wales: Tony Swift at Swansea, Colin Smart at Newport and John Scott at Cardiff.

— ENGLAND LEGENDS: DAVID DUCKHAM —

Equally adept at wing or centre, 'Dai' Duckham retired from international rugby in 1976 as England's second highest career try scorer after Cyril Lowe. Duckham's achievement was all the more remarkable considering that he played for the most part in an unsuccessful England team, which 'won' four wooden spoons during his seven-year career.

Duckham had more opportunities to show just how good he was when he was supported by a better class of player in the British Lions and Barbarians teams. With the Lions in New Zealand in 1971, he scored a then record six tries in a touring match in Greymouth; while, playing for the Barbarians against the All Blacks in Cardiff in 1974, he ghosted past five defenders to set up the winning try for J.P.R. Williams.

Nicknamed 'Quackers', Duckham played for Coventry for many years and skippered his club to successive John Player Cup wins in 1973 and 1974.

'Dai' Duckham

David John Duckham Factfile
Born: 28 Jun 1946 in Coventry, Warwickshire
Club: Coventry
Caps: 36 (W11, D2, L23)
Scoring: 10 tries – 36 pts
England debut: 8 Feb 1969 vs Ireland (Dublin)

— WHISTLE BLOWERS —

Strange as it seems now, the first six England tests did not feature a referee. Early international matches were conducted with two umpires, one nominated by each side, who patrolled the touchlines and ensured that the match was played within the laws. It wasn't until 1875 that the referee joined the players on the pitch.

Irish referee Mr Abram Combe was the first man to take charge of an England game, having whistle-blowing duties for the visit to Lansdowne Road on 13 December 1875. The first neutral referee to officiate at an England game was Mr H.L. Robinson of Ireland for the match against Scotland at Manchester on 4 March 1882.

Mr Chisholm Robson was the first southern hemisphere whistler to take charge of an England match, doing so for the encounter with his home country, New Zealand, at Eden Park, Auckland on 25 May 1963. The first French referee, Bernard Marie, followed for Ireland's visit to Twickenham in 1966.

Argentina's Pablo Deluca is still the only referee from outside the Five Nations and Tri-Nations to take charge of an England game – doing so on four occasions: against Italy at Twickenham in 1996, Romania at Twickenham in 2001, Wales in Cardiff 2003 and Georgia at Perth in 2003.

— WOODEN SPOON —

The 'wooden spoon' was originally associated with the Cambridge University Mathematical Tripos exams, and was a kind of booby prize awarded by students to their lowest ranked class-mate in the final exams.

How the wooden spoon idea transferred to rugby union is not exactly known. However, in the early years of the International Championship there were many Cambridge graduates among the players, some of whom may have attempted to preserve the concept after the last academic wooden spoon was awarded in 1909.

Nowadays the wooden spoon is 'awarded' to the team finishing bottom of the table in the Six Nations Championship. Sadly for those who relish the humiliation of others, the least successful captain has never been presented with an actual wooden spoon.

However, such is the stigma of the wooden spoon that the 'winners' will sometimes claim that it should only be awarded to a team winning no games at all – although this exalted level of incompetence is properly known as a 'whitewash'.

England have claimed the wooden spoon on 14 occasions with just two of those being whitewashes: in 1972 and 1976.

— ALL CHANGE —

On only one occasion in England history have all 15 players in the starting line-up been different to the ones who began the previous test. The match in question was the World Cup warm-up match against Wales at the Millennium Stadium, Cardiff on 23 August 2003 which coach Clive Woodward used to blood new players and try out different combinations. The previous game had seen a totally different XV start against Australia in Melbourne two months earlier.

21 June 2003		23 August 2003	
Australia (Won 25–14)		*Wales (Won 43–9)*	
15	Josh Lewsey	15	Dan Scarbrough
14	Jason Robinson	14	James Simpson-Daniel
13	Will Greenwood	13	Jamie Noon
12	Mike Tindall	12	Stuart Abbott
11	Ben Cohen	11	Dan Luger
10	Jonny Wilkinson	10	Alex King
9	Kyran Bracken	9	Andy Gomarsall
1	Trevor Woodman	1	Jason Leonard (capt)
2	Steve Thompson	2	Mark Regan
3	Phil Vickery	3	Julian White
4	Martin Johnson (capt)	4	Danny Grewcock
5	Ben Kay	5	Simon Shaw
6	Richard Hill	6	Martin Corry
7	Neil Back	7	Lewis Moody
8	Lawrence Dallaglio	8	Joe Worsley

— ENGLAND AT THE FIFTH RUGBY WORLD CUP: 2003 —

Games and Scorers:
Pool C

12 Oct	Georgia Perth	W 84–6	t: Greenwood 2, Cohen 2, Tindall, Dawson, Thompson, Back, Dallaglio, Regan, Robinson, Luger. c: Wilkinson 5, Grayson 4. p: Wilkinson 2
18 Oct	S Africa Perth	W 25–6	t: Greenwood. c: Wilkinson. p: Wilkinson 4. d: Wilkinson 2

26 Oct	Samoa	Melbourne	W 35–22	t: Back, Balshaw, Vickery, penalty try. c: Wilkinson 3. p: Wilkinson 2. d: Wilkinson
2 Nov	Uruguay	Brisbane	W 111–13	t: Lewsey 5, Balshaw 2, Gomarsall 2, Robinson 2, Catt 2, Moody, Luger, Abbott, Greenwood. c: Grayson 11, Catt 2

RWC Pool C Table:

Nation	P	W	D	L	F	A	Pts	Tries
England	4	4	0	0	255	47	19	34
South Africa	4	3	0	1	184	60	15	27
Samoa	4	2	0	2	138	117	10	18
Uruguay	4	1	0	3	56	255	4	6
Georgia	4	0	0	4	46	200	0	1

Quarter-final

9 Nov	Wales	Brisbane	W 28–17	t: Greenwood. c: Wilkinson. p: Wilkinson 6. d: Wilkinson

Semi-Final

16 Nov	France	Sydney	W 24–7	p: Wilkinson 5. d: Wilkinson 3

Final

22 Nov	Australia	Sydney	W 20–17*	t: Robinson. p: Wilkinson 4. d: Wilkinson

* After Extra Time

Squad and Appearances:
Head Coach: Clive Woodward. Coach: Andy Robinson.
Captain: Martin Johnson.
Stuart Abbott (London Wasps) Sm/Ur/W(r); Neil Back (Leicester Tigers) G/SA/Sm/W/F/Au; Iain Balshaw (Bath) Sm/Ur/Au(r); Kyran Bracken (Saracens) SA/Ur(r)/W(r)/F(r); Mike Catt (Bath) Sm(r)/Ur/W(r)/F/Au(r); Ben Cohen (Northampton Saints) G/SA/Sm/W/F/Au; Martin Corry (Leicester Tigers) Ur; Lawrence Dallaglio (London Wasps) G/SA/Sm/Ur/W/F/Au; Matt Dawson (Northampton Saints)

G/Sm/W/F/Au; Andy Gomarsall (Gloucester) G(r)/Ur; Paul Grayson (Northampton Saints) G(r)/Ur; Will Greenwood (NEC Harlequins) G/SA/Ur(r)/W/F/Au; Danny Grewcock (Bath) Ur; Richard Hill (Saracens) G/F/Au; Martin Johnson (Leicester Tigers) G/SA/Sm/Ur(r)/W/F/Au; Ben Kay (Leicester Tigers) G/SA/Sm/W/F/Au; Jason Leonard (NEC Harlequins) G(r)/SA(r)/Sm/Ur/W/F(r)/Au(r); Josh Lewsey (London Wasps) G/SA/Ur/F/Au; Dan Luger (Perpignan) G(r)/SA(r)/Ur/W; Lewis Moody (Leicester Tigers) G(r)/SA/Sm(r)/Ur/W/F(r)/Au(r); Mark Regan (Leeds Tykes) G(r)/Sm; Jason Robinson (Sale Sharks) G/SA/Sm/Ur(r)/W/F/Au; Simon Shaw (London Wasps); Steve Thompson (Northampton Saints) G/SA/Sm(r)/W/F/Au; Mike Tindall (Bath) G/SA/Sm/W/F(r)/Au; Phil Vickery (Gloucester) G/SA/Sm(r)/Ur/W/F/Au; Dorian West (Leicester Tigers) Ur/F(r); Julian White (Leicester Tigers) Sm/Ur(r); Jonny Wilkinson (Newcastle Falcons) G/SA/Sm/W/F/Au; Trevor Woodman (Gloucester) G/SA/W(r)/F/Au; Joe Worsley (London Wasps) SA(r)/Sm/Ur.

Phil Vickery was captain against Uruguay. Appearances as a replacement marked with (r).

Scoring:

Name	T	C	P	D	Pts
Jonny Wilkinson	-	10	23	8	113
Paul Grayson	-	15	-	-	30
Will Greenwood	5	-	-	-	25
Josh Lewsey	5	-	-	-	25
Jason Robinson	4	-	-	-	20
Iain Balshaw	3	-	-	-	15
Mike Catt	2	2	-	-	14
Neil Back	2	-	-	-	10
Ben Cohen	2	-	-	-	10
Andy Gomarsall	2	-	-	-	10
Dan Luger	2	-	-	-	10
Stuart Abbott	1	-	-	-	5
Lawrence Dallaglio	1	-	-	-	5
Matt Dawson	1	-	-	-	5
Lewis Moody	1	-	-	-	5
Mark Regan	1	-	-	-	5
Steve Thompson	1	-	-	-	5
Mike Tindall	1	-	-	-	5
Phil Vickery	1	-	-	-	5
Penalty Try	1	-	-	-	5
TOTALS	**36**	**27**	**23**	**8**	**327**
AGAINST	**7**	**4**	**15**	**0**	**88**

— ENGLAND LEGENDS: DEAN RICHARDS —

Dean Richards, England's most capped No. 8, marked his arrival on the international stage by scoring two tries against Ireland in 1986, a feat not achieved by an England player on his debut for 57 years. Blessed with immense strength and an uncanny 'nose' for the ball, Richards was always the rock at the centre of any England team he played for.

Richards was selected to play in the inaugural World Cup competition in 1987, appearing in all England's games. He also featured in the following two World Cup campaigns: in 1991 playing in the first three pool games; and, in 1995, he recovered from injury to play in the knock-out stages.

He represented his country in a total of nine Five Nations tournaments, which included three Grand Slams (1991, 1992 and 1995) and a further Five Nations Championship triumph in 1996.

Richards spent six years as Leicester Tigers' director of rugby after 17 seasons with the club as a player spanning both the amateur and professional eras. He was involved in all Leicester's league title wins: as a player in 1988, as captain in 1995 and as director of rugby for the four consecutive Premiership titles 1999–2002. He was also the tactical brains behind Leicester's back-to-back European Cup victories of 2001 and 2002 and their inaugural Zurich Championship victory.

He was awarded an MBE in the 1996 New Year's Honours list, and is now director of rugby at Harlequins.

Dean Richards MBE Factfile
Born: 11 Jul 1963 in Nuneaton, Warwickshire
Clubs: Roanne (France), Leicester
Caps: 48 (W35, D1, L12)
Scoring: 6 tries – 24 pts
England debut: 1 Mar 1986 vs Ireland (Twickenham)

— VICTORIA CROSS —

The only English rugby union international to have been awarded the Victoria Cross is Arthur Leyland Harrison, a Lieutenant-Commander aboard *HMS Lion* during World War I. Harrison, who had won two caps in 1914 at the age of 28, fought at the battle of Jutland and was mentioned in dispatches in 1916. He lost his life in April 1918 during the second day of the blockade of Zeebrugge. 588 British soldiers and sailors lost their lives on the same say as Harrison, who was awarded the VC posthumously.

The *London Gazette* of 14 March 1919 reported: "For most

conspicuous gallantry at Zeebrugge on the night of the 22–23 April 1918. This officer was in immediate command of the Naval Storming Parties embarked in *(HMS) Vindictive.* Immediately before coming alongside the Mole Lieut.-Commander Harrison was struck on the head by a fragment of a shell which broke his jaw and knocked him senseless. Recovering consciousness he proceeded on to the Mole and took over command of his party, who were attacking the seaward end of the Mole. The silencing of the guns on the Mole head was of the first importance, and though in a position fully exposed to the enemy's machine-gun fire Lieut.-Commander Harrison gathered his men together and led them to the attack. He was killed at the head of his men, all of whom were either killed or wounded. Lieut.-Commander Harrison, though already severely wounded and undoubtedly in great pain, displayed indomitable resolution and courage of the highest order in pressing his attack, knowing as he did that any delay in silencing the guns might jeopardise the main object of the expedition, i.e., the blocking of the Zeebrugge-Bruges Canal."

— ENGLAND AT THE SIXTH RUGBY WORLD CUP: 2007 —

Games & Scorers:
Pool A

8 Sep	USA	Lens	W 28–10	t: Robinson, Barkley, Rees. c: Barkley 2. p: Barkley 3
14 Sep	S Africa	Paris	L 0–36	
22 Sep	Samoa	Nantes	W 44–22	t: Sackey 2, Corry 2. c: Wilkinson 3. p: Wilkinson 4. d: Wilkinson 2
28 Sep	Tonga	Paris	W 36–20	t: Sackey 2, Tait, Farrell. c: Wilkinson 2. p: Wilkinson 2. d: Wilkinson 2

RWC Pool A Table:

Nation	P	W	D	L	F	A	Pts	Tries
South Africa	4	4	0	0	189	47	19	24
England	4	3	0	1	108	88	14	11
Tonga	4	2	0	2	89	96	9	9
Samoa	4	1	0	3	69	143	5	5
USA	4	0	0	4	61	142	1	7

Quarter-final

6 Oct   Australia   Marseille   W 12–10   p: Wilkinson 4

Semi-Final

13 Oct   France   Paris   W 14–9   t: Lewsey. p:
                                            Wilkinson 2.
                                            d: Wilkinson

Final

20 Oct   S Africa   Paris   L 6–15   p: Wilkinson 2

Squad & Appearances:

Head Coach: Brian Ashton. Coach: John Wells. Captain: Phil Vickery. Nick Abendanon (Bath); Olly Barkley (Bath) US/Sm/T; Steve Borthwick (Bath) SA(r)/Sm(r)/T; Mike Catt (London Irish) US/SA/Au/F/SA; George Chuter (Leicester Tigers) US(r)/SA(r)/Sm/T/Au(r)/F(r)/SA(r); Martin Corry (Leicester Tigers) US(r)/SA/Sm/T/Au/F/SA; Mark Cueto (Sale Sharks) US/Sm/T/SA; Lawrence Dallaglio (London Wasps) US/T(r)/Au(r)/F(r)/SA(r); Nick Easter (Harlequins) SA/Sm/T/Au/F/SA; Andy Farrell (Saracens) US(r)/SA/T(r); Toby Flood (Newcastle Falcons) Au(r)/F(r)/SA(r); Perry Freshwater (Perpignan) SA(r)/Sm(r); Andy Gomarsall (Harlequins) SA(r)/Sm/T/Au/F/SA; Dan Hipkiss (Leicester Tigers) Sm(r)/T(r)/F(r)/SA(r); Ben Kay (Leicester Tigers) US/SA/Sm/T/Au/F/SA; Josh Lewsey (London Wasps) US/SA/Sm/T/Au/F; Lee Mears (Bath) T(r); Lewis Moody (Leicester Tigers) US(r)/SA(r)/Sm(r)/T/Au/F/SA; Jamie Noon (Newcastle Falcons) US/SA; Shaun Perry (Bristol) US/SA; Tom Rees (London Wasps) US/SA; Mark Regan (Bristol) US/SA/Au/F/SA; Peter Richards (London Irish) US(r)/SA(r)/T(r)/Au(r)/F(r)/SA(r); Jason Robinson (unattached) US/SA/Au/F/SA; Paul Sackey (London Wasps) SA/Sm/T/Au/F/SA; Simon Shaw (London Wasps) US/SA/Sm/Au/F/SA; Andrew Sheridan (Sale Sharks) US/SA/Sm/T/Au/F/SA; Matt Stevens (Bath) US(r)/SA/Sm/T/Au(r)/F(r)/SA(r); Mathew Tait (Newcastle Falcons) US(r)/SA(r)/Sm/T/Au/F/SA; Phil Vickery (London Wasps) US/T(r)/Au/F/SA; Jonny Wilkinson (Newcastle Falcons) Sm/T/Au/F/SA; Joe Worsley (London Wasps) US/Sm/Au(r)/F(r)/SA(r).

* Due to injuries, Flood replaced Lewsey and Abendanon replaced Noon in the squad.

Martin Corry was captain for the pool matches against South Africa, Samoa and Tonga.

Appearances as a replacement marked with (r).

Scoring:

Name	T	C	P	D	Pts
Jonny Wilkinson	-	5	14	5	67
Paul Sackey	4	-	-	-	20
Olly Barkley	1	2	3	-	18
Martin Corry	2	-	-	-	10
Andy Farrell	1	-	-	-	5
Josh Lewsey	1	-	-	-	5
Tom Rees	1	-	-	-	5
Jason Robinson	1	-	-	-	5
Mathew Tait	1	-	-	-	5
TOTALS	12	7	17	5	140
AGAINST	8	8	22	0	122

— ENGLAND LEGENDS: WAVELL WAKEFIELD —

One of the outstanding players of his generation, Wavell Wakefield was as adept at centre or at lock as in his normal back-row position. He was also one of the leading thinkers about the game, credited with introducing the greater specialisation among the forwards that developed in the 1920s. During this period Wakefield wrote two instructional and semi-autobiographical books, *Rugger* and *Rugger – how to play it*. He led England to their 1924 Grand Slam and his total of 31 caps remained an England record for 43 years until surpassed by Budge Rogers.

Wakefield left school in 1916 and saw active service during World War I in the Royal Naval Air Service (later the Fleet Air Arm), before transferring to the Royal Flying Corps. He was mentioned in dispatches, and rose to the rank of captain. He retired from the RAF in 1923 but continued active flying in the reserve and in 1939 he was appointed director of the Air Training Corps.

After retiring from the game he became a referee but although he reached the international panel, he never officiated an international game. He became RFU president in 1950–51 and was a member of the International Rugby Football Board from 1954 until 1961.

Wakefield also enjoyed a successful political career. From 1935 until 1945 he was the Conservative MP for Swindon, receiving a knighthood in 1944 "for political and public services". He subsequently represented the Marylebone Division from 1945 to 1963, when he was made the first Baron Wakefield of Kendal.

*Wavell Wakefield: war hero, author,
England international and RFU President*

William Wavell Wakefield Factfile
Born: 10 Mar 1898 in Beckenham, London
Clubs: Leicester, Furness, Harlequins
Caps: 31 (W20, D3, L8)
Scoring: 6 tries – 18 pts
England debut: 17 Jan 1920 vs Wales (Swansea)

— YOUNG GUNS/OLD HANDS —

When Mike Catt ran out at centre against Wales in 2007 he became the oldest player to occupy that position for England. The complete list of youngest and oldest players at each position:

Position	Youngest	Oldest
Full-back	Marshall Brooks (v Sco 1874), 18	Fred Gilbert (v Ire 1923), 38
Wing	Wilfrid Lowry (v Fra 1920), 19	Frank Sykes (v Aus 1963), 35
Centre	Mathew Tait (v Wal 2005), 18	Mike Catt (v Wal 2007), 35
Fly-half	Colin Laird (v Wal 1927), 18	Les Cusworth (v Wal 1988), 33**
Scrum-half	George Marsden (v Wal 1900), 19	Richard Harding (v Fiji 1988), 34
Prop	Dick Stafford (v Wal 1912), 18	Colin White (v Fra 1984), 36*
Hooker	Alfred Maynard (v Wal 1914), 19	Eric Evans (v Sco 1958), 37
Lock	Fenton Smith (v Wal 1910), 19	John Fidler (v Saf 1984), 35
Flanker	Bryan West (v Wal 1968m), 19	Neil Back (v Aus 2003), 34
No 8	David Gay (v Wal 1968), 19	Bob Hesford (v Wal 1985), 34

* Paul Rendall was 37 years of age when coming on as a replacement against Italy in 1991.
** Rob Andrew was 34 when a replacement fly-half against Wales in 1997.

— ENGLAND'S RESULTS 1871–2008 —

A complete list of England's 608 official test match results.
England's record in those matches is won 323, lost 237 drawn 48. They have scored 9,432 points from 1,314 tries, 741 conversions, 908 penalty goals, 124 drop goals plus 4 goals from a mark.

Key

RWC	Rugby World Cup	(2)	2nd Test
WCQ	World Cup Qualifier	(qf)	Quarter-final
4NC	Four Nations Championship	(sf)	Semi-final
5NC	Five Nations Championship	(f)	Final
6NC	Six Nations Championship	(3/4)	3rd & 4th Place Playoff
CKC	Cook Cup	(po)	Play-off
(1)	1st Test	*	After extra time

No	Date	Opponents	Tourny	Venue	Result
1	27 Mar 1871	Scotland		Edinburgh	Lost 1t-1g,1t
2	5 Feb 1872	Scotland		Kennington Oval	Won 1g,1dg,2t-1dg
3	3 Mar 1873	Scotland		Glasgow	Drew 0–0
4	23 Feb 1874	Scotland		Kennington Oval	Won 1dg-1t
5	15 Feb 1875	Ireland		Kennington Oval	Won 1g,1dg,1t-0
6	8 Mar 1875	Scotland		Edinburgh	Drew 0–0
7	13 Dec 1875	Ireland		Dublin	Won 1g,1t-0
8	6 Mar 1876	Scotland		Kennington Oval	Won 1g,1t-0
9	5 Feb 1877	Ireland		Kennington Oval	Won 2g,2t-0
10	5 Mar 1877	Scotland		Edinburgh	Lost 0–1dg
11	4 Mar 1878	Scotland		Kennington Oval	Drew 0–0
12	11 Mar 1878	Ireland		Dublin	Won 2g,1t-0
13	10 Mar 1879	Scotland		Edinburgh	Drew 1g-1dg
14	24 Mar 1879	Ireland		Kennington Oval	Won 2g,1dg,2t-0
15	30 Jan 1880	Ireland		Dublin	Won 1g,1t-1t
16	28 Feb 1880	Scotland		Manchester	Won 2g,3t-1g
17	5 Feb 1881	Ireland		Manchester	Won 2g,2t-0
18	19 Feb 1881	Wales		Blackheath	Won 7g,1dg,6t-0

No	Date	Opponents	Tourny	Venue	Result
19	19 Mar 1881	Scotland		Edinburgh	Drew 1dg,1t-1g,1t
20	6 Feb 1882	Ireland		Dublin	Drew 2t-2t
21	4 Mar 1882	Scotland		Manchester	Lost 0–2t
22	16 Dec 1882	Wales	4NC	Swansea	Won 2g,4t-0
23	5 Feb 1883	Ireland	4NC	Manchester	Won 1g,3t-0
24	3 Mar 1883	Scotland	4NC	Edinburgh	Won 2t-1t
25	5 Jan 1884	Wales	4NC	Leeds	Won 1g,2t-1g
26	4 Feb 1884	Ireland	4NC	Dublin	Won 1g-0
27	1 Mar 1884	Scotland	4NC	Blackheath	Won 1g-1t
28	3 Jan 1885	Wales	4NC	Swansea	Won 1g,4t-1g,1t
29	7 Feb 1885	Ireland	4NC	Manchester	Won 2t-1t
30	2 Jan 1886	Wales	4NC	Blackheath	Won 1gm,2t-1g
31	6 Feb 1886	Ireland	4NC	Dublin	Won 1t-0
32	13 Mar 1886	Scotland	4NC	Edinburgh	Drew 0–0
33	8 Jan 1887	Wales	4NC	Llanelli	Drew 0–0
34	5 Feb 1887	Ireland	4NC	Dublin	Lost 0–2g
35	5 Mar 1887	Scotland	4NC	Manchester	Drew 1t-1t
36	16 Feb 1889	NZ Natives		Blackheath	Won 7–0
37	15 Feb 1890	Wales	4NC	Dewsbury	Lost 0–1
38	1 Mar 1890	Scotland	4NC	Edinburgh	Won 6–0
39	15 Mar 1890	Ireland	4NC	Blackheath	Won 3–0
40	3 Jan 1891	Wales	4NC	Newport	Won 7–3
41	7 Feb 1891	Ireland	4NC	Dublin	Won 9–0
42	7 Mar 1891	Scotland	4NC	Richmond	Lost 3–9
43	2 Jan 1892	Wales	4NC	Blackheath	Won 17–0
44	6 Feb 1892	Ireland	4NC	Manchester	Won 7–0
45	5 Mar 1892	Scotland	4NC	Edinburgh	Won 5–0
46	7 Jan 1893	Wales	4NC	Cardiff	Lost 11–12
47	4 Feb 1893	Ireland	4NC	Dublin	Won 4–0
48	4 Mar 1893	Scotland	4NC	Leeds	Lost 0–8
49	6 Jan 1894	Wales	4NC	Birkenhead Park	Won 24–3
50	3 Feb 1894	Ireland	4NC	Blackheath	Lost 5–7
51	17 Mar 1894	Scotland	4NC	Edinburgh	Lost 0–6
52	5 Jan 1895	Wales	4NC	Swansea	Won 14–6
53	2 Feb 1895	Ireland	4NC	Dublin	Won 6–3
54	9 Mar 1895	Scotland	4NC	Richmond	Lost 3–6
55	4 Jan 1896	Wales	4NC	Blackheath	Won 25–0
56	1 Feb 1896	Ireland	4NC	Leeds	Lost 4–10
57	14 Mar 1896	Scotland	4NC	Glasgow	Lost 0–11
58	9 Jan 1897	Wales	4NC	Newport	Lost 0–11
59	6 Feb 1897	Ireland	4NC	Dublin	Lost 9–13
60	13 Mar 1897	Scotland	4NC	Manchester	Won 12–3
61	5 Feb 1898	Ireland	4NC	Richmond	Lost 6–9
62	12 Mar 1898	Scotland	4NC	Edinburgh	Drew 3–3
63	2 Apr 1898	Wales	4NC	Blackheath	Won 14–7
64	7 Jan 1899	Wales	4NC	Swansea	Lost 3–26

No	Date	Opponents	Tourny	Venue	Result
65	4 Feb 1899	Ireland	4NC	Dublin	Lost 0–6
66	11 Mar 1899	Scotland	4NC	Blackheath	Lost 0–5
67	6 Jan 1900	Wales	4NC	Gloucester	Lost 3–13
68	3 Feb 1900	Ireland	4NC	Richmond	Won 15–4
69	10 Mar 1900	Scotland	4NC	Inverleith	Drew 0–0
70	5 Jan 1901	Wales	4NC	Cardiff	Lost 0–13
71	9 Feb 1901	Ireland	4NC	Dublin	Lost 6–10
72	9 Mar 1901	Scotland	4NC	Blackheath	Lost 3–18
73	11 Jan 1902	Wales	4NC	Blackheath	Lost 8–9
74	8 Feb 1902	Ireland	4NC	Leicester	Won 6–3
75	15 Mar 1902	Scotland	4NC	Inverleith	Won 6–3
76	10 Jan 1903	Wales	4NC	Swansea	Lost 5–21
77	14 Feb 1903	Ireland	4NC	Dublin	Lost 0–6
78	21 Mar 1903	Scotland	4NC	Richmond	Lost 6–10
79	9 Jan 1904	Wales	4NC	Leicester	Drew 14–14
80	13 Feb 1904	Ireland	4NC	Blackheath	Won 19–0
81	19 Mar 1904	Scotland	4NC	Inverleith	Lost 3–6
82	14 Jan 1905	Wales	4NC	Cardiff	Lost 0–25
83	11 Feb 1905	Ireland	4NC	Cork	Lost 3–17
84	18 Mar 1905	Scotland	4NC	Richmond	Lost 0–8
85	2 Dec 1905	New Zealand		Crystal Palace	Lost 0–15
86	13 Jan 1906	Wales	4NC	Richmond	Lost 3–16
87	10 Feb 1906	Ireland	4NC	Leicester	Lost 6–16
88	17 Mar 1906	Scotland	4NC	Inverleith	Won 9–3
89	22 Mar 1906	France		Paris	Won 35–8
90	8 Dec 1906	South Africa		Crystal Palace	Drew 3–3
91	5 Jan 1907	France		Richmond	Won 41–13
92	12 Jan 1907	Wales	4NC	Swansea	Lost 0–22
93	9 Feb 1907	Ireland	4NC	Dublin	Lost 9–17
94	16 Mar 1907	Scotland	4NC	Blackheath	Lost 3–8
95	1 Jan 1908	France		Paris	Won 19–0
96	18 Jan 1908	Wales	4NC	Bristol	Lost 18–28
97	8 Feb 1908	Ireland	4NC	Richmond	Won 13–3
98	21 Mar 1908	Scotland	4NC	Inverleith	Lost 10–16
99	9 Jan 1909	Australia		Blackheath	Lost 3–9
100	16 Jan 1909	Wales	4NC	Cardiff	Lost 0–8
101	30 Jan 1909	France		Leicester	Won 22–0
102	13 Feb 1909	Ireland	4NC	Dublin	Won 11–5
103	20 Mar 1909	Scotland	4NC	Richmond	Lost 8–18
104	15 Jan 1910	Wales	5NC	Twickenham	Won 11–6
105	12 Feb 1910	Ireland	5NC	Twickenham	Drew 0–0
106	3 Mar 1910	France	5NC	Paris	Won 11–3
107	19 Mar 1910	Scotland	5NC	Inverleith	Won 14–5
108	21 Jan 1911	Wales	5NC	Swansea	Lost 11–15
109	28 Jan 1911	France	5NC	Twickenham	Won 37–0
110	11 Feb 1911	Ireland	5NC	Dublin	Lost 0–3
111	18 Mar 1911	Scotland	5NC	Twickenham	Won 13–8
112	20 Jan 1912	Wales	5NC	Twickenham	Won 8–0

No	Date	Opponents	Tourny	Venue	Result
113	10 Feb 1912	Ireland	5NC	Twickenham	Won 15–0
114	16 Mar 1912	Scotland	5NC	Inverleith	Lost 3–8
115	8 Apr 1912	France	5NC	Paris	Won 18–8
116	4 Jan 1913	South Africa		Twickenham	Lost 3–9
117	18 Jan 1913	Wales	5NC	Cardiff	Won 12–0
118	25 Jan 1913	France	5NC	Twickenham	Won 20–0
119	8 Feb 1913	Ireland	5NC	Dublin	Won 15–4
120	15 Mar 1913	Scotland	5NC	Twickenham	Won 3–0
121	17 Jan 1914	Wales	5NC	Twickenham	Won 10–9
122	14 Feb 1914	Ireland	5NC	Twickenham	Won 17–12
123	21 Mar 1914	Scotland	5NC	Inverleith	Won 16–15
124	13 Apr 1914	France	5NC	Paris	Won 39–13
125	17 Jan 1920	Wales	5NC	Swansea	Lost 5–19
126	31 Jan 1920	France	5NC	Twickenham	Won 8–3
127	14 Feb 1920	Ireland	5NC	Dublin	Won 14–11
128	20 Mar 1920	Scotland	5NC	Twickenham	Won 13–4
129	15 Jan 1921	Wales	5NC	Twickenham	Won 18–3
130	12 Feb 1921	Ireland	5NC	Twickenham	Won 15–0
131	19 Mar 1921	Scotland	5NC	Inverleith	Won 18–0
132	28 Mar 1921	France	5NC	Paris	Won 10–6
133	21 Jan 1922	Wales	5NC	Cardiff	Lost 6–28
134	11 Feb 1922	Ireland	5NC	Dublin	Won 12–3
135	25 Feb 1922	France	5NC	Twickenham	Drew 11–11
136	18 Mar 1922	Scotland	5NC	Twickenham	Won 11–5
137	20 Jan 1923	Wales	5NC	Twickenham	Won 7–3
138	10 Feb 1923	Ireland	5NC	Leicester	Won 23–5
139	17 Mar 1923	Scotland	5NC	Inverleith	Won 8–6
140	2 Apr 1923	France	5NC	Paris	Won 12–3
141	19 Jan 1924	Wales	5NC	Swansea	Won 17–9
142	9 Feb 1924	Ireland	5NC	Belfast	Won 14–3
143	23 Feb 1924	France	5NC	Twickenham	Won 19–7
144	15 Mar 1924	Scotland	5NC	Twickenham	Won 19–0
145	3 Jan 1925	New Zealand		Twickenham	Lost 11–17
146	17 Jan 1925	Wales	5NC	Twickenham	Won 12–6
147	14 Feb 1925	Ireland	5NC	Twickenham	Drew 6–6
148	21 Mar 1925	Scotland	5NC	Edinburgh	Lost 11–14
149	13 Apr 1925	France	5NC	Paris	Won 13–11
150	16 Jan 1926	Wales	5NC	Cardiff	Drew 3–3
151	13 Feb 1926	Ireland	5NC	Dublin	Lost 15–19
152	27 Feb 1926	France	5NC	Twickenham	Won 11–0
153	20 Mar 1926	Scotland	5NC	Twickenham	Lost 9–17
154	15 Jan 1927	Wales	5NC	Twickenham	Won 11–9
155	12 Feb 1927	Ireland	5NC	Twickenham	Won 8–6
156	19 Mar 1927	Scotland	5NC	Edinburgh	Lost 13–21
157	2 Apr 1927	France	5NC	Paris	Lost 0–3
158	7 Jan 1928	Australia		Twickenham	Won 18–11
159	21 Jan 1928	Wales	5NC	Swansea	Won 10–8
160	11 Feb 1928	Ireland	5NC	Dublin	Won 7–6
161	25 Feb 1928	France	5NC	Twickenham	Won 18–8

No	Date	Opponents	Tourny	Venue	Result
162	17 Mar 1928	Scotland	5NC	Twickenham	Won 6–0
163	19 Jan 1929	Wales	5NC	Twickenham	Won 8–3
164	9 Feb 1929	Ireland	5NC	Twickenham	Lost 5–6
165	16 Mar 1929	Scotland	5NC	Edinburgh	Lost 6–12
166	1 Apr 1929	France	5NC	Paris	Won 16–6
167	18 Jan 1930	Wales	5NC	Cardiff	Won 11–3
168	8 Feb 1930	Ireland	5NC	Dublin	Lost 3–4
169	22 Feb 1930	France	5NC	Twickenham	Won 11–5
170	15 Mar 1930	Scotland	5NC	Twickenham	Drew 0–0
171	17 Jan 1931	Wales	5NC	Twickenham	Drew 11–11
172	14 Feb 1931	Ireland	5NC	Twickenham	Lost 5–6
173	21 Mar 1931	Scotland	5NC	Edinburgh	Lost 19–28
174	6 Apr 1931	France	5NC	Paris	Lost 13–14
175	2 Jan 1932	South Africa		Twickenham	Lost 0–7
176	16 Jan 1932	Wales	4NC	Swansea	Lost 5–12
177	13 Feb 1932	Ireland	4NC	Dublin	Won 11–8
178	19 Mar 1932	Scotland	4NC	Twickenham	Won 16–3
179	21 Jan 1933	Wales	4NC	Twickenham	Lost 3–7
180	11 Feb 1933	Ireland	4NC	Twickenham	Won 17–6
181	18 Mar 1933	Scotland	4NC	Edinburgh	Lost 0–3
182	20 Jan 1934	Wales	4NC	Cardiff	Won 9–0
183	10 Feb 1934	Ireland	4NC	Dublin	Won 13–3
184	17 Mar 1934	Scotland	4NC	Twickenham	Won 6–3
185	19 Jan 1935	Wales	4NC	Twickenham	Drew 3–3
186	9 Feb 1935	Ireland	4NC	Twickenham	Won 14–3
187	16 Mar 1935	Scotland	4NC	Edinburgh	Lost 7–10
188	4 Jan 1936	New Zealand		Twickenham	Won 13–0
189	18 Jan 1936	Wales	4NC	Swansea	Drew 0–0
190	8 Feb 1936	Ireland	4NC	Dublin	Lost 3–6
191	21 Mar 1936	Scotland	4NC	Twickenham	Won 9–8
192	16 Jan 1937	Wales	4NC	Twickenham	Won 4–3
193	13 Feb 1937	Ireland	4NC	Twickenham	Won 9–8
194	20 Mar 1937	Scotland	4NC	Edinburgh	Won 6–3
195	15 Jan 1938	Wales	4NC	Cardiff	Lost 8–14
196	12 Feb 1938	Ireland	4NC	Dublin	Won 36–14
197	19 Mar 1938	Scotland	4NC	Twickenham	Lost 16–21
198	21 Jan 1939	Wales	4NC	Twickenham	Won 3–0
199	11 Feb 1939	Ireland	4NC	Twickenham	Lost 0–5
200	18 Mar 1939	Scotland	4NC	Edinburgh	Won 9–6
201	18 Jan 1947	Wales	5NC	Cardiff	Won 9–6
202	8 Feb 1947	Ireland	5NC	Dublin	Lost 0–22
203	15 Mar 1947	Scotland	5NC	Twickenham	Won 24–5
204	19 Apr 1947	France	5NC	Twickenham	Won 6–3
205	3 Jan 1948	Australia		Twickenham	Lost 0–11
206	17 Jan 1948	Wales	5NC	Twickenham	Drew 3–3
207	14 Feb 1948	Ireland	5NC	Twickenham	Lost 10–11
208	20 Mar 1948	Scotland	5NC	Edinburgh	Lost 3–6
209	29 Mar 1948	France	5NC	Paris	Lost 0–15
210	15 Jan 1949	Wales	5NC	Cardiff	Lost 3–9

No	Date	Opponents	Tourny	Venue	Result
211	12 Feb 1949	Ireland	5NC	Dublin	Lost 5–14
212	26 Feb 1949	France	5NC	Twickenham	Won 8–3
213	19 Mar 1949	Scotland	5NC	Twickenham	Won 19–3
214	21 Jan 1950	Wales	5NC	Twickenham	Lost 5–11
215	11 Feb 1950	Ireland	5NC	Twickenham	Won 3–0
216	25 Feb 1950	France	5NC	Paris	Lost 3–6
217	18 Mar 1950	Scotland	5NC	Edinburgh	Lost 11–13
218	20 Jan 1951	Wales	5NC	Swansea	Lost 5–23
219	10 Feb 1951	Ireland	5NC	Dublin	Lost 0–3
220	24 Feb 1951	France	5NC	Twickenham	Lost 3–11
221	17 Mar 1951	Scotland	5NC	Twickenham	Won 5–3
222	5 Jan 1952	South Africa		Twickenham	Lost 3–8
223	19 Jan 1952	Wales	5NC	Twickenham	Lost 6–8
224	15 Mar 1952	Scotland	5NC	Edinburgh	Won 19–3
225	29 Mar 1952	Ireland	5NC	Twickenham	Won 3–0
226	5 Apr 1952	France	5NC	Paris	Won 6–3
227	17 Jan 1953	Wales	5NC	Cardiff	Won 8–3
228	14 Feb 1953	Ireland	5NC	Dublin	Drew 9–9
229	28 Feb 1953	France	5NC	Twickenham	Won 11–0
230	21 Mar 1953	Scotland	5NC	Twickenham	Won 26–8
231	16 Jan 1954	Wales	5NC	Twickenham	Won 9–6
232	30 Jan 1954	New Zealand		Twickenham	Lost 0–5
233	13 Feb 1954	Ireland	5NC	Twickenham	Won 14–3
234	20 Mar 1954	Scotland	5NC	Edinburgh	Won 13–3
235	10 Apr 1954	France	5NC	Paris	Lost 3–11
236	22 Jan 1955	Wales	5NC	Cardiff	Lost 0–3
237	12 Feb 1955	Ireland	5NC	Dublin	Drew 6–6
238	26 Feb 1955	France	5NC	Twickenham	Lost 9–16
239	19 Mar 1955	Scotland	5NC	Twickenham	Won 9–6
240	21 Jan 1956	Wales	5NC	Twickenham	Lost 3–8
241	11 Feb 1956	Ireland	5NC	Twickenham	Won 20–0
242	17 Mar 1956	Scotland	5NC	Edinburgh	Won 11–6
243	14 Apr 1956	France	5NC	Paris	Lost 9–14
244	19 Jan 1957	Wales	5NC	Cardiff	Won 3–0
245	9 Feb 1957	Ireland	5NC	Dublin	Won 6–0
246	23 Feb 1957	France	5NC	Twickenham	Won 9–5
247	16 Mar 1957	Scotland	5NC	Twickenham	Won 16–3
248	18 Jan 1958	Wales	5NC	Twickenham	Drew 3–3
249	1 Feb 1958	Australia		Twickenham	Won 9–6
250	8 Feb 1958	Ireland	5NC	Twickenham	Won 6–0
251	1 Mar 1958	France	5NC	Paris	Won 14–0
252	15 Mar 1958	Scotland	5NC	Edinburgh	Drew 3–3
253	17 Jan 1959	Wales	5NC	Cardiff	Lost 0–5
254	14 Feb 1959	Ireland	5NC	Dublin	Won 3–0
255	28 Feb 1959	France	5NC	Twickenham	Drew 3–3
256	21 Mar 1959	Scotland	5NC	Twickenham	Drew 3–3
257	16 Jan 1960	Wales	5NC	Twickenham	Won 14–6
258	13 Feb 1960	Ireland	5NC	Twickenham	Won 8–5

No	Date	Opponents	Tourny	Venue	Result
259	27 Feb 1960	France	5NC	Paris	Drew 3–3
260	19 Mar 1960	Scotland	5NC	Edinburgh	Won 21–12
261	7 Jan 1961	South Africa		Twickenham	Lost 0–5
262	21 Jan 1961	Wales	5NC	Cardiff	Lost 3–6
263	11 Feb 1961	Ireland	5NC	Dublin	Lost 8–11
264	25 Feb 1961	France	5NC	Twickenham	Drew 5–5
265	18 Mar 1961	Scotland	5NC	Twickenham	Won 6–0
266	20 Jan 1962	Wales	5NC	Twickenham	Drew 0–0
267	10 Feb 1962	Ireland	5NC	Twickenham	Won 16–0
268	24 Feb 1962	France	5NC	Paris	Lost 0–13
269	17 Mar 1962	Scotland	5NC	Edinburgh	Drew 3–3
270	19 Jan 1963	Wales	5NC	Cardiff	Won 13–6
271	9 Feb 1963	Ireland	5NC	Dublin	Drew 0–0
272	23 Feb 1963	France	5NC	Twickenham	Won 6–5
273	16 Mar 1963	Scotland	5NC	Twickenham	Won 10–8
274	25 May 1963	New Zealand(1)		Auckland	Lost 11–21
275	1 Jun 1963	New Zealand(2)		Christchurch	Lost 6–9
276	4 Jun 1963	Australia		Sydney	Lost 9–18
277	4 Jan 1964	New Zealand		Twickenham	Lost 0–14
278	18 Jan 1964	Wales	5NC	Twickenham	Drew 6–6
279	8 Feb 1964	Ireland	5NC	Twickenham	Lost 5–18
280	22 Feb 1964	France	5NC	Paris	Won 6–3
281	21 Mar 1964	Scotland	5NC	Edinburgh	Lost 6–15
282	16 Jan 1965	Wales	5NC	Cardiff	Lost 3–14
283	13 Feb 1965	Ireland	5NC	Dublin	Lost 0–5
284	27 Feb 1965	France	5NC	Twickenham	Won 9–6
285	20 Mar 1965	Scotland	5NC	Twickenham	Drew 3–3
286	15 Jan 1966	Wales	5NC	Twickenham	Lost 6–11
287	12 Feb 1966	Ireland	5NC	Twickenham	Drew 6–6
288	26 Feb 1966	France	5NC	Paris	Lost 0–13
289	7 Jan 1967	Scotland	5NC	Edinburgh	Lost 3–6
290	7 Jan 1967	Australia		Twickenham	Lost 11–23
291	11 Feb 1967	Ireland	5NC	Dublin	Won 8–3
292	25 Feb 1967	France	5NC	Twickenham	Lost 12–16
293	18 Mar 1967	Scotland	5NC	Twickenham	Won 27–14
294	15 Apr 1967	Wales	5NC	Cardiff	Lost 21–34
295	4 Nov 1967	New Zealand		Twickenham	Lost 11–23
296	20 Jan 1968	Wales	5NC	Twickenham	Drew 11–11
297	10 Feb 1968	Ireland	5NC	Twickenham	Drew 9–9
298	24 Feb 1968	France	5NC	Paris	Lost 9–14
299	16 Mar 1968	Scotland	5NC	Edinburgh	Won 8–6
300	8 Feb 1969	Ireland	5NC	Dublin	Lost 15–17
301	22 Feb 1969	France	5NC	Twickenham	Won 22–8
302	15 Mar 1969	Scotland	5NC	Twickenham	Won 8–3
303	12 Apr 1969	Wales	5NC	Cardiff	Lost 9–30
304	20 Dec 1969	South Africa		Twickenham	Won 11–8
305	14 Feb 1970	Ireland	5NC	Twickenham	Won 9–3

No	Date	Opponents	Tourny	Venue	Result
306	28 Feb 1970	Wales	5NC	Twickenham	Lost 13–17
307	21 Mar 1970	Scotland	5NC	Edinburgh	Lost 5–14
308	18 Apr 1970	France	5NC	Paris	Lost 13–35
309	16 Jan 1971	Wales	5NC	Cardiff	Lost 6–22
310	13 Feb 1971	Ireland	5NC	Dublin	Won 9–6
311	27 Feb 1971	France	5NC	Twickenham	Drew 14–14
312	20 Mar 1971	Scotland	5NC	Twickenham	Lost 15–16
313	27 Mar 1971	Scotland		Edinburgh	Lost 6–26
314	17 Apr 1971	President's XV		Twickenham	Lost 11–28
315	15 Jan 1972	Wales	5NC	Twickenham	Lost 3–12
316	12 Feb 1972	Ireland	5NC	Twickenham	Lost 12–16
317	26 Feb 1972	France	5NC	Paris	Lost 12–37
318	18 Mar 1972	Scotland	5NC	Edinburgh	Lost 9–23
319	3 Jun 1972	South Africa		Johannesburg	Won 18–9
320	6 Jan 1973	New Zealand		Twickenham	Lost 0–9
321	20 Jan 1973	Wales	5NC	Cardiff	Lost 9–25
322	10 Feb 1973	Ireland	5NC	Dublin	Lost 9–18
323	24 Feb 1973	France	5NC	Twickenham	Won 14–6
324	17 Mar 1973	Scotland	5NC	Twickenham	Won 20–13
325	15 Sep 1973	New Zealand		Auckland	Won 16–10
326	17 Nov 1973	Australia		Twickenham	Won 20–3
327	2 Feb 1974	Scotland	5NC	Edinburgh	Lost 14–16
328	16 Feb 1974	Ireland	5NC	Twickenham	Lost 21–26
329	2 Mar 1974	France	5NC	Paris	Drew 12–12
330	16 Mar 1974	Wales	5NC	Twickenham	Won 16–12
331	18 Jan 1975	Ireland	5NC	Dublin	Lost 9–12
332	1 Feb 1975	France	5NC	Twickenham	Lost 20–27
333	15 Feb 1975	Wales	5NC	Cardiff	Lost 4–20
334	15 Mar 1975	Scotland	5NC	Twickenham	Won 7–6
335	24 May 1975	Australia(1)		Sydney	Lost 9–16
336	31 May 1975	Australia (2)		Brisbane	Lost 21–30
337	3 Jan 1976	Australia		Twickenham	Won 23–6
338	17 Jan 1976	Wales	5NC	Twickenham	Lost 9–21
339	21 Feb 1976	Scotland	5NC	Edinburgh	Lost 12–22
340	6 Mar 1976	Ireland	5NC	Twickenham	Lost 12–13
341	20 Mar 1976	France	5NC	Paris	Lost 9–30
342	15 Jan 1977	Scotland	5NC	Twickenham	Won 26–6
343	5 Feb 1977	Ireland	5NC	Dublin	Won 4–0
344	19 Feb 1977	France	5NC	Twickenham	Lost 3–4
345	5 Mar 1977	Wales	5NC	Cardiff	Lost 9–14
346	21 Jan 1978	France	5NC	Paris	Lost 6–15
347	4 Feb 1978	Wales	5NC	Twickenham	Lost 6–9
348	4 Mar 1978	Scotland	5NC	Edinburgh	Won 15–0
349	18 Mar 1978	Ireland	5NC	Twickenham	Won 15–9
350	25 Nov 1978	New Zealand		Twickenham	Lost 6–16
351	3 Feb 1979	Scotland	5NC	Twickenham	Drew 7–7
352	17 Feb 1979	Ireland	5NC	Dublin	Lost 7–12
353	3 Mar 1979	France	5NC	Twickenham	Won 7–6
354	17 Mar 1979	Wales	5NC	Cardiff	Lost 3–27

No	Date	Opponents	Tourny	Venue	Result
355	24 Nov 1979	New Zealand		Twickenham	Lost 9–10
356	19 Jan 1980	Ireland	5NC	Twickenham	Won 24–9
357	2 Feb 1980	France	5NC	Paris	Won 17–13
358	16 Feb 1980	Wales	5NC	Twickenham	Won 9–8
359	15 Mar 1980	Scotland	5NC	Edinburgh	Won 30–18
360	17 Jan 1981	Wales	5NC	Cardiff	Lost 19–21
361	21 Feb 1981	Scotland	5NC	Twickenham	Won 23–17
362	7 Mar 1981	Ireland	5NC	Dublin	Won 10–6
363	21 Mar 1981	France	5NC	Twickenham	Lost 12–16
364	30 May 1981	Argentina (1)		Buenos Aires	Drew 19–19
365	6 Jun 1981	Argentina (2)		Buenos Aires	Won 12–6
366	2 Jan 1982	Australia		Twickenham	Won 15–11
367	16 Jan 1982	Scotland	5NC	Edinburgh	Drew 9–9
368	6 Feb 1982	Ireland	5NC	Twickenham	Lost 15–16
369	20 Feb 1982	France	5NC	Paris	Won 27–15
370	6 Mar 1982	Wales	5NC	Twickenham	Won 17–7
371	15 Jan 1983	France	5NC	Twickenham	Lost 15–19
372	5 Feb 1983	Wales	5NC	Cardiff	Drew 13–13
373	5 Mar 1983	Scotland	5NC	Twickenham	Lost 12–22
374	19 Mar 1983	Ireland	5NC	Dublin	Lost 15–25
375	19 Nov 1983	New Zealand		Twickenham	Won 15–9
376	4 Feb 1984	Scotland	5NC	Edinburgh	Lost 6–18
377	18 Feb 1984	Ireland	5NC	Twickenham	Won 12–9
378	3 Mar 1984	France	5NC	Paris	Lost 18–32
379	17 Mar 1984	Wales	5NC	Twickenham	Lost 15–24
380	2 Jun 1984	South Africa(1)		Port Elizabeth	Lost 15–33
381	9 Jun 1984	South Africa(2)		Johannesburg	Lost 9–35
382	3 Nov 1984	Australia		Twickenham	Lost 3–19
383	5 Jan 1985	Romania		Twickenham	Won 22–15
384	2 Feb 1985	France	5NC	Twickenham	Drew 9–9
385	16 Mar 1985	Scotland	5NC	Twickenham	Won 10–7
386	30 Mar 1985	Ireland	5NC	Dublin	Lost 10–13
387	20 Apr 1985	Wales	5NC	Cardiff	Lost 15–24
388	1 Jun 1985	New Zealand(1)		Christchurch	Lost 13–18
389	8 Jun 1985	New Zealand(2)		Wellington	Lost 15–42
390	18 Jan 1986	Wales	5NC	Twickenham	Won 21–18
391	15 Feb 1986	Scotland	5NC	Edinburgh	Lost 6–33
392	1 Mar 1986	Ireland	5NC	Twickenham	Won 25–20
393	15 Mar 1986	France	5NC	Paris	Lost 10–29
394	7 Feb 1987	Ireland	5NC	Dublin	Lost 0–17
395	21 Feb 1987	France	5NC	Twickenham	Lost 15–19
396	7 Mar 1987	Wales	5NC	Cardiff	Lost 12–19
397	4 Apr 1987	Scotland	5NC	Twickenham	Won 21–12
398	23 May 1987	Australia	RWC	Sydney	Lost 6–19
399	30 May 1987	Japan	RWC	Sydney	Won 60–7
400	3 Jun 1987	United States	RWC	Sydney	Won 34–6
401	8 Jun 1987	Wales(qf)	RWC	Brisbane	Lost 3–16

No	Date	Opponents	Tourny	Venue	Result
402	16 Jan 1988	France	5NC	Paris	Lost 9–10
403	6 Feb 1988	Wales	5NC	Twickenham	Lost 3–11
404	5 Mar 1988	Scotland	5NC	Edinburgh	Won 9–6
405	19 Mar 1988	Ireland	5NC	Twickenham	Won 35–3
406	23 Apr 1988	Ireland		Dublin	Won 21–10
407	29 May 1988	Australia(1)		Brisbane	Lost 16–22
408	12 Jun 1988	Australia (2)		Sydney	Lost 8–28
409	16 Jun 1988	Fiji		Suva	Won 25–12
410	5 Nov 1988	Australia		Twickenham	Won 28–19
411	4 Feb 1989	Scotland	5NC	Twickenham	Drew 12–12
412	18 Feb 1989	Ireland	5NC	Dublin	Won 16–3
413	4 Mar 1989	France	5NC	Twickenham	Won 11–0
414	18 Mar 1989	Wales	5NC	Cardiff	Lost 9–12
415	13 May 1989	Romania		Bucharest	Won 58–3
416	4 Nov 1989	Fiji		Twickenham	Won 58–23
417	20 Jan 1990	Ireland	5NC	Twickenham	Won 23–0
418	3 Feb 1990	France	5NC	Paris	Won 26–7
419	17 Feb 1990	Wales	5NC	Twickenham	Won 34–6
420	17 Mar 1990	Scotland	5NC	Edinburgh	Lost 7–13
421	28 Jul 1990	Argentina (1)		Buenos Aires	Won 25–12
422	4 Aug 1990	Argentina (2)		Buenos Aires	Lost 13–15
423	3 Nov 1990	Argentina		Twickenham	Won 51–0
424	19 Jan 1991	Wales	5NC	Cardiff	Won 25–6
425	16 Feb 1991	Scotland	5NC	Twickenham	Won 21–12
426	2 Mar 1991	Ireland	5NC	Dublin	Won 16–7
427	16 Mar 1991	France	5NC	Twickenham	Won 21–19
428	20 Jul 1991	Fiji		Suva	Won 28–12
429	27 Jul 1991	Australia		Sydney	Lost 15–40
430	3 Oct 1991	New Zealand	RWC	Twickenham	Lost 12–18
431	8 Oct 1991	Italy	RWC	Twickenham	Won 36–6
432	11 Oct 1991	United States	RWC	Twickenham	Won 37–9
433	19 Oct 1991	France(qf)	RWC	Paris	Won 19–10
434	26 Oct 1991	Scotland(sf)	RWC	Edinburgh	Won 9–6
435	2 Nov 1991	Australia(f)	RWC	Twickenham	Lost 6–12
436	18 Jan 1992	Scotland	5NC	Edinburgh	Won 25–7
437	1 Feb 1992	Ireland	5NC	Twickenham	Won 38–9
438	15 Feb 1992	France	5NC	Paris	Won 31–13
439	7 Mar 1992	Wales	5NC	Twickenham	Won 24–0
440	17 Oct 1992	Canada		Wembley Stadium	Won 26–13
441	14 Nov 1992	South Africa		Twickenham	Won 33–16
442	16 Jan 1993	France	5NC	Twickenham	Won 16–15
443	6 Feb 1993	Wales	5NC	Cardiff	Lost 9–10
444	6 Mar 1993	Scotland	5NC	Twickenham	Won 26–12
445	20 Mar 1993	Ireland	5NC	Dublin	Lost 3–17
446	27 Nov 1993	New Zealand		Twickenham	Won 15–9
447	5 Feb 1994	Scotland	5NC	Edinburgh	Won 15–14
448	19 Feb 1994	Ireland	5NC	Twickenham	Lost 12–13
449	5 Mar 1994	France	5NC	Paris	Won 18–14
450	19 Mar 1994	Wales	5NC	Twickenham	Won 15–8

No	Date	Opponents	Tourny	Venue	Result
451	4 Jun 1994	South Africa(1)		Pretoria	Won 32–15
452	11 Jun 1994	South Africa(2)		Cape Town	Lost 9–27
453	12 Nov 1994	Romania		Twickenham	Won 54–3
454	10 Dec 1994	Canada		Twickenham	Won 60–19
455	21 Jan 1995	Ireland	5NC	Dublin	Won 20–8
456	4 Feb 1995	France	5NC	Twickenham	Won 31–10
457	18 Feb 1995	Wales	5NC	Cardiff	Won 23–9
458	18 Mar 1995	Scotland	5NC	Twickenham	Won 24–12
459	27 May 1995	Argentina	RWC	Durban	Won 24–18
460	31 May 1995	Italy	RWC	Durban	Won 27–20
461	4 Jun 1995	Samoa	RWC	Durban	Won 44–22
462	11 Jun 1995	Australia (qf)	RWC	Cape Town	Won 25–22
463	18 Jun 1995	New Zealand(sf)	RWC	Cape Town	Lost 29–45
464	22 Jun 1995	France (3/4)	RWC	Pretoria	Lost 9–19
465	18 Nov 1995	South Africa		Twickenham	Lost 14–24
466	16 Dec 1995	Samoa		Twickenham	Won 27–9
467	20 Jan 1996	France	5NC	Paris	Lost 12–15
468	3 Feb 1996	Wales	5NC	Twickenham	Won 21–15
469	2 Mar 1996	Scotland	5NC	Edinburgh	Won 18–9
470	16 Mar 1996	Ireland	5NC	Twickenham	Won 28–15
471	23 Nov 1996	Italy		Twickenham	Won 54–21
472	14 Dec 1996	Argentina		Twickenham	Won 20–18
473	1 Feb 1997	Scotland	5NC	Twickenham	Won 41–13
474	15 Feb 1997	Ireland	5NC	Dublin	Won 46–6
475	1 Mar 1997	France	5NC	Twickenham	Lost 20–23
476	15 Mar 1997	Wales	5NC	Cardiff	Won 34–13
477	31 May 1997	Argentina (1)		Buenos Aires	Won 46–20
478	7 Jun 1997	Argentina (2)		Buenos Aires	Lost 13–33
479	12 Jul 1997	Australia	CKC	Sydney	Lost 6–25
480	15 Nov 1997	Australia	CKC	Twickenham	Drew 15–15
481	22 Nov 1997	New Zealand(1)		Manchester	Lost 8–25
482	29 Nov 1997	South Africa		Twickenham	Lost 11–29
483	6 Dec 1997	New Zealand(2)		Twickenham	Drew 26–26
484	7 Feb 1998	France	5NC	Paris	Lost 17–24
485	21 Feb 1998	Wales	5NC	Twickenham	Won 60–26
486	22 Mar 1998	Scotland	5NC	Edinburgh	Won 34–20
487	4 Apr 1998	Ireland	5NC	Twickenham	Won 35–17
488	6 Jun 1998	Australia	CKC	Brisbane	Lost 0–76
489	20 Jun 1998	New Zealand(1)		Dunedin	Lost 22–64
490	27 Jun 1998	New Zealand(2)		Auckland	Lost 10–40
491	4 Jul 1998	South Africa		Cape Town	Lost 0–18
492	14 Nov 1998	Netherlands	WCQ	Huddersfield	Won 110–0
493	22 Nov 1998	Italy	WCQ	Huddersfield	Won 23–15
494	28 Nov 1998	Australia	CKC	Twickenham	Lost 11–12
495	5 Dec 1998	South Africa		Twickenham	Won 13–7
496	20 Feb 1999	Scotland	5NC	Twickenham	Won 24–21
497	6 Mar 1999	Ireland	5NC	Dublin	Won 27–15

No	Date	Opponents	Tourny	Venue	Result
498	20 Mar 1999	France	5NC	Twickenham	Won 21–10
499	11 Apr 1999	Wales	5NC	Wembley Stadium	Lost 31–32
500	26 Jun 1999	Australia	CKC	Sydney	Lost 15–22
501	21 Aug 1999	United States		Twickenham	Won 106–8
502	28 Aug 1999	Canada		Twickenham	Won 36–11
503	2 Oct 1999	Italy	RWC	Twickenham	Won 67–7
504	9 Oct 1999	New Zealand	RWC	Twickenham	Lost 16–30
505	15 Oct 1999	Tonga	RWC	Twickenham	Won 101–10
506	20 Oct 1999	Fiji(po)	RWC	Twickenham	Won 45–24
507	24 Oct 1999	South Africa(qf)	RWC	Paris	Lost 21–44
508	5 Feb 2000	Ireland	6NC	Twickenham	Won 50–18
509	19 Feb 2000	France	6NC	Paris	Won 15–9
510	4 Mar 2000	Wales	6NC	Twickenham	Won 46–12
511	18 Mar 2000	Italy	6NC	Rome	Won 59–12
512	2 Apr 2000	Scotland	6NC	Edinburgh	Lost 13–19
513	17 Jun 2000	South Africa(1)		Pretoria	Lost 13–18
514	24 Jun 2000	South Africa(2)		Bloemfontein	Won 27–22
515	18 Nov 2000	Australia	CKC	Twickenham	Won 22–19
516	25 Nov 2000	Argentina		Twickenham	Won 19–0
517	2 Dec 2000	South Africa		Twickenham	Won 25–17
518	3 Feb 2001	Wales	6NC	Cardiff	Won 44–15
519	17 Feb 2001	Italy	6NC	Twickenham	Won 80–23
520	3 Mar 2001	Scotland	6NC	Twickenham	Won 43–3
521	7 Apr 2001	France	6NC	Twickenham	Won 48–19
522	2 Jun 2001	Canada(1)		Markham	Won 22–10
523	9 Jun 2001	Canada(2)		Burnaby	Won 59–20
524	16 Jun 2001	United States		San Francisco	Won 48–19
525	20 Oct 2001	Ireland	6NC	Dublin	Lost 14–20
526	10 Nov 2001	Australia	CKC	Twickenham	Won 21–15
527	17 Nov 2001	Romania		Twickenham	Won 134–0
528	24 Nov 2001	South Africa		Twickenham	Won 29–9
529	2 Feb 2002	Scotland	6NC	Edinburgh	Won 29–3
530	16 Feb 2002	Ireland	6NC	Twickenham	Won 45–11
531	2 Mar 2002	France	6NC	Paris	Lost 15–20
532	23 Mar 2002	Wales	6NC	Twickenham	Won 50–10
533	7 Apr 2002	Italy	6NC	Rome	Won 45–9
534	22 Jun 2002	Argentina		Buenos Aires	Won 26–18
535	9 Nov 2002	New Zealand		Twickenham	Won 31–28
536	16 Nov 2002	Australia	CKC	Twickenham	Won 32–31
537	23 Nov 2002	South Africa		Twickenham	Won 53–3
538	15 Feb 2003	France	6NC	Twickenham	Won 25–17
539	22 Feb 2003	Wales	6NC	Cardiff	Won 26–9
540	9 Mar 2003	Italy	6NC	Twickenham	Won 40–5
541	22 Mar 2003	Scotland	6NC	Twickenham	Won 40–9
542	30 Mar 2003	Ireland	6NC	Dublin	Won 42–6
543	14 Jun 2003	New Zealand		Wellington	Won 15–13
544	21 Jun 2003	Australia	CKC	Melbourne	Won 25–14
545	23 Aug 2003	Wales		Cardiff	Won 43–9
546	30 Aug 2003	France		Marseille	Lost 16–17

No	Date	Opponents	Tourny	Venue	Result
547	6 Sep 2003	France		Twickenham	Won 45–14
548	12 Oct 2003	Georgia	RWC	Perth	Won 84–6
549	18 Oct 2003	South Africa	RWC	Perth	Won 25–6
550	26 Oct 2003	Samoa	RWC	Melbourne	Won 35–22
551	2 Nov 2003	Uruguay	RWC	Brisbane	Won 111–13
552	9 Nov 2003	Wales(qf)	RWC	Brisbane	Won 28–17
553	16 Nov 2003	France(sf)	RWC	Sydney	Won 24–7
554	22 Nov 2003	Australia(f)	RWC	Sydney	Won 20–17*
555	15 Feb 2004	Italy	6NC	Rome	Won 50–9
556	21 Feb 2004	Scotland	6NC	Edinburgh	Won 35–13
557	6 Mar 2004	Ireland	6NC	Twickenham	Lost 13–19
558	20 Mar 2004	Wales	6NC	Twickenham	Won 31–21
559	27 Mar 2004	France	6NC	Paris	Lost 21–24
560	12 Jun 2004	New Zealand(1)		Dunedin	Lost 3–36
561	19 Jun 2004	New Zealand(2)		Auckland	Lost 12–36
562	26 Jun 2004	Australia	CKC	Brisbane	Lost 15–51
563	13 Nov 2004	Canada		Twickenham	Won 70–0
564	20 Nov 2004	South Africa		Twickenham	Won 32–16
565	27 Nov 2004	Australia	CKC	Twickenham	Lost 19–21
566	5 Feb 2005	Wales	6NC	Cardiff	Lost 9–11
567	13 Feb 2005	France	6NC	Twickenham	Lost 17–18
568	27 Feb 2005	Ireland	6NC	Dublin	Lost 13–19
569	12 Mar 2005	Italy	6NC	Twickenham	Won 39–7
570	19 Mar 2005	Scotland	6NC	Twickenham	Won 43–22
571	12 Nov 2005	Australia	CKC	Twickenham	Won 26–16
572	19 Nov 2005	New Zealand		Twickenham	Lost 19–23
573	26 Nov 2005	Samoa		Twickenham	Won 40–3
574	4 Feb 2006	Wales	6NC	Twickenham	Won 47–13
575	11 Feb 2006	Italy	6NC	Rome	Won 31–16
576	25 Feb 2006	Scotland	6NC	Edinburgh	Lost 12–18
577	12 Mar 2006	France	6NC	Paris	Lost 6–31
578	18 Mar 2006	Ireland	6NC	Twickenham	Lost 24–28
579	11 Jun 2006	Australia(1)	CKC	Sydney	Lost 3–34
580	17 Jun 2006	Australia(2)	CKC	Melbourne	Lost 18–43
581	5 Nov 2006	New Zealand		Twickenham	Lost 20–41
582	11 Nov 2006	Argentina		Twickenham	Lost 18–25
583	18 Nov 2006	South Africa (1)		Twickenham	Won 23–21
584	25 Nov 2006	South Africa(2)		Twickenham	Lost 14–25
585	3 Feb 2007	Scotland	6NC	Twickenham	Won 42–20
586	10 Feb 2007	Italy	6NC	Twickenham	Won 20–7
587	24 Feb 2007	Ireland	6NC	Dublin	Lost 13–43
588	11 Mar 2007	France	6NC	Twickenham	Won 26–18
589	17 Mar 2007	Wales	6NC	Cardiff	Lost 18–27
590	26 May 2007	South Africa (1)		Bloemfontein	Lost 10–58
591	2 Jun 2007	South Africa (2)		Pretoria	Lost 22–55
592	4 Aug 2007	Wales		Twickenham	Won 62–5
593	11 Aug 2007	France		Twickenham	Lost 15–21
594	18 Aug 2007	France		Marseille	Lost 9–22
595	8 Sep 2007	United States	RWC	Lens	Won 28–10

No	Date	Opponents	Tourny	Venue	Result
596	14 Sep 2007	South Africa	RWC	Paris	Lost 0–36
597	22 Sep 2007	Samoa	RWC	Nantes	Won 44–22
598	28 Sep 2007	Tonga	RWC	Paris	Won 36–20
599	6 Oct 2007	Australia(qf)	RWC	Marseille	Won 12–10
600	13 Oct 2007	France(sf)	RWC	Paris	Won 14–9
601	20 Oct 2007	South Africa(f)	RWC	Paris	Lost 6–15
602	2 Feb 2008	Wales	6NC	Twickenham	Lost 19–26
603	10 Feb 2008	Italy	6NC	Rome	Won 23–19
604	23 Feb 2008	France	6NC	Paris	Won 24–13
605	8 Mar 2008	Scotland	6NC	Edinburgh	Lost 9–15
606	15 Mar 2008	Ireland	6NC	Twickenham	Won 33–10
607	14 Jun 2008	New Zealand(1)		Auckland	Lost 20–37
608	21 Jun 2008	New Zealand(2)		Christchurch	Lost 12–44